GLOBETROTTER
TRAVEL GUIDES

SOUTH AFRICA

PETER JOYCE

NEW
HOLLAND

GLOBETROTTER

TRAVEL GUIDES

First edition published in 1994 by
New Holland (Publishers) Ltd
London • Cape Town • Sydney

Copyright © 1994 in text: Peter Joyce
Copyright © 1994 in maps: Globetrotter
Travel Maps
Copyright © 1994 in photographs: Individual photographers as credited below.
Copyright © 1994 New Holland (Publishers) Ltd

ISBN 1 85368 365 5

New Holland (Publishers) Ltd
37 Connaught Street, London W2 2AZ

Editor: Mariëlle Renssen
Assistant Editors: Tracey Hawthorne,
Angela Sayer-Farley
Designer: Neville Poulter
Cartography: Globetrotter Travel Maps

Typeset by Struik DTP
Reproduction by Hirt & Carter (Pty) Ltd,
Cape Town
Printed and bound in Singapore by Tien Wah Press
(Pte) Ltd

Acknowledgements: The publishers wish to thank
the following for their co-operation with the photographers involved in this project: Blydepoort
Resort, the KwaZulu Department of Nature
Conservation, the Oceanarium in Port Elizabeth,
the Natal Parks Board, the National Parks Board
and Sun International.

Photographic credits: **Shaen Adey**, pages 7, 25, 36,
71, 73, 78, 79, 82, 88, 117; **Gerald Cubitt**, pages 4,
19, 21, 22, 23, 28, 37, 92; **Roger de la Harpe**, cover
(top left and bottom left), title page, pages 26 (top
right), 77, 98; **Nigel Dennis**, cover (top right), pages
11, 55, 58; **Walter Knirr**, cover (bottom right), pages
14, 15, 26 (bottom right), 30, 34, 35, 38, 39, 41, 42, 43,
46, 49, 50, 51, 52, 62, 65, 66, 67, 68, 69, 72, 74, 75, 102,
105, 108, 109, 110, 111, 112, 115, 116 (top); **John
McKinnell**, page 87; **Nicola Newman**, page 27;
Marek Patzer, page 26 (bottom left); **Struik Image
Library/Erhardt Thiel**, pages 26 (top left), 29, 106,
107, 113, 114; **Struik Image Library/Peter Pickford**,
pages 6, 8, 10, 53, 54, 56, 57, 59, 95, 97, 116 (bottom),
118, 119; **The Argus Newspaper**, page 17; **Colin
Urquhart**, pages 86, 99; **Mark van Aardt**, pages
16, 89, 96; **Lanz von Hörsten**, page 94; **Keith
Young**, page 85.

CONTENTS

1
Introducing
South Africa

South Africa covers an area of well over a million square kilometres (386,000 square miles) – a size three times larger than unified Germany, or almost equal to Texas, California and Alabama combined.

In human terms, it's an extremely diverse country: the contrasts are strikingly apparent in the bewildering mix of race and language, creed, colour and culture.

Variety is there, too, in the character of the cities and the nature of the land. Travel eastwards from the modern metropolis of **Johannesburg** and you'll get to the mistily beautiful **Transvaal escarpment**; below this is the heat-hazed Lowveld plain and its world-famous **Kruger National Park**, one of the largest and most successful conservation areas in the world, attracting over 700,000 visitors annually. As enticing to the visitor is the more tropical eastern coastal region of **Natal**, with its splendid **Zululand** game reserves, along with the towering heights of the **Drakensberg** mountains, and **Durban**, its golden beaches stretching to far horizons on either side. The spectacular **Transkei** coast, wild and unspoilt, lies farther south, and beyond, along the Cape's southern shores, is the exquisite **Garden Route**.

Finally, almost at the southern tip of the continent there is **Cape Town**, set beneath the awesome buttress of the **Table Mountain** chain; the scenic **Peninsula** and its memorable coastal drives; and the neighbouring **Winelands** – a magical combination of hills and emerald valleys, vineyards, orchards and historic homesteads.

South Africa is truly a world in one country.

TOP ATTRACTIONS

*** Kruger National Park
One of the world's largest wildlife conservation areas.
*** Cape Town
The Cape Peninsula's most visited features are Table Mountain and Cape Point.
*** Lost City at Sun City
A pleasure-seeker's dream, 1·5 hrs from Johannesburg.
** The Garden Route
South Africa's Eden stretches 200 km (125 miles) along the southern Cape coast.
** Northern Natal
Offers fun in the sun and the splendid Zululand game reserves.
** The Drakensberg
Breathtaking views from this towering massif, 200 km (125 miles) inland of Durban.

Opposite: *The golden sands of Plettenberg Bay.*

FACTS AND FIGURES

- **Highest mountain** is Champagne Castle; at 3,348 m (10,990 ft), it is just one of many tall peaks in the main wall of the Drakensberg mountain range.
- **Longest river** is the Orange, which flows for some 2,250 km (1,400 miles) from east to west.
- **Largest waterfall** (and one of the world's six largest) is the Augrabies on the Orange River; in full spate it comprises 19 cataracts tumbling 92 m (300 ft).
- **Deepest gorge**: Blyde River Canyon in the Eastern Transvaal is up to 800 m (2,625 ft) deep and 1·5 km (1 mile) wide in places.

THE LAND

In broad geophysical terms, South Africa can be divided into just two regions: the great, semicircular interior plateau, and the generally narrow coastal belt that fringes the plateau on three sides. A third distinctive feature is the division between the two – the continuous necklace of mountains and hills known as the **Great Escarpment**. Much of the interior is taken up by the **Karoo**, a huge, flattish semi-desert that covers around 400,000 square kilometres (154,440 square miles) of the **Cape Province** and some of the **Orange Free State**. Beyond, to the northeast, the land rises to the **Highveld**, whose towns – among them **Johannesburg** and **Pretoria** – lie almost 1,500 metres (4,920 feet) above sea level.

The eastern regions of the country have a kinder climate, richer soils and lusher vegetation than the western parts, and it is here that you'll find most of the cities and towns – and the largest concentrations of people.

Mountains and Rivers

The country's most impressive mountains are those of the **Drakensberg**, the spectacular eastern part of the Great Escarpment, whose gigantic basalt faces fall almost sheer for a full 2,000 metres (6,565 feet) to the green Natal midlands. So formidable is this range that the main 250-kilometre (155 miles) stretch can only be crossed by the **Sani Pass**, which winds its tortuous way up into the kingdom of Lesotho.

Formed by a quite different geological process are the Cape fold mountains, running parallel to the southern coast. Here, the **Swartberg** and **Tsitsikamma**, the **Outeniqua** and **Langeberg**, rise majestically over the Little Karoo and Garden Route, their grand heights cut through by some of the most dramatic of passes. Inland from Cape Town, the striking **Hottentots-Holland** and the

Below: *The lower reaches of the Orange, South Africa's largest river.*
Right: *The Wolfberg Arch is one of the Cedarberg's many dramatic wind-sculpted rock formations.*

Drakenstein mountain ranges grace the lovely wine-lands. And then, of course, there's world-renowned **Table Mountain** and its great sandstone buttresses towering over the city of Cape Town. To the northwest, the rugged **Cedarberg** is home to the rare Clanwilliam cedar and the pure-white snow protea (*Protea cryophila*).

A number of the country's rivers rise in the Natal Drakensberg, eight alone on the aptly named **Mont-aux-Sources** (mountain of springs) massif. Many of these tumble down the eastern slopes, to discharge eventually into the Indian Ocean.

South Africa's largest watercourse, the **Orange River**, also rises in the area, but flows west across the country and finally plunges through the Augrabies gorge, close to the Namibian border, before starting its last, desolate stretch to the Atlantic. Though much of its course crosses arid, treeless terrain, its waters are increasingly being used to irrigate the flanking farmlands.

Other significant rivers include the **Vaal**, a tributary of the Orange, the Western Cape's **Olifants** and beautiful **Berg**, the **Breede** in the Southwestern Cape, the **Sundays** and **Great Fish** in the Eastern Cape, and the **Limpopo** to the north (marking South Africa's border with Zimbabwe).

For all that, though, South Africa's rivers do not amount to very much in world terms. Put together, their total run-off is barely equal to that of the Rhine at Rotterdam, and to just half that of the mighty Zambezi 1,000 kilometres (620 miles) to the north.

Seas and Shores

The country's coastline presents a strik-ing study in contrasts. The western seaboard is a barren region of rocky, windblown shores and waters chilled by the **Benguela Current**. It does, however, have its attractions: a wealth of seabirds (huge colonies of gannets, cormorants and terns roost and nest on the offshore

---

RIVER RAFTING: ALL THE RAGE

A popular way to enjoy the beauty and excitement of South Africa's rivers is to join a group of river rafters or canoeists. No experience is necessary as experts are at hand to show you the ropes and ensure your safety and comfort. It is best to join a party organized by one of the five or six reputable opera-tors. Trips lasting between one and four days negotiate stretches of the following major watercourses:

● **Orange River**, which runs through the Northern Cape and along the Namibian border

● **Breede River** near Swellendam in the South-western Cape; one operator includes a wine-tasting ses-sion in the itinerary!

● **Tugela River**, which flows over some challenging rapids in central Natal

● **Sabie River** in the lovely Eastern Transvaal (rafting on this watercourse is subject to seasonal rains).

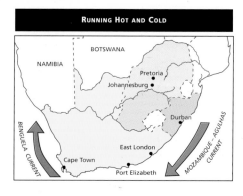

RUNNING HOT AND COLD

The south and east coasts, on the other hand, are washed by the warmer waters of the **Mozambique-Agulhas Current**, and in tourist terms are a lot more popular. In the south, the 220-kilometre (135 miles) Garden Route, stretching roughly from Mossel Bay to the Storms River is an especially beautiful green and forested coastal terrace overlooked by splendid mountains. Equally enticing to holiday-makers are the wide expanses of golden sand and the sun-drenched resort villages to either side of Durban.

The Mkambati Nature Reserve in Transkei, on the country's southeastern shoreline, is a paradise for both the fisherman and the botanist: the area is sliced through by rivers and forested ravines; exquisite wildflowers mantle the hillsides.

islands), charming fishing villages, tasty rock lobsters on dinner tables, and, for a few brief springtime weeks, a countryside magically transformed by great carpets of wild flowers.

Climate

Weather patterns, dictated by ocean currents, altitude, prevailing winds and the ever-changing nature of the land, vary dramatically from place to place.

When it comes to rainfall, though, the divisions are simple and clear. The southwestern tip of South Africa, centring on the lovely city of **Cape Town**, has a Mediterranean climate with winter rain (May to August), while the **southern Cape** and the **Natal** coasts experience **showers** all year round. These are heavy – almost tropical – in Natal, especially in summer. Over much of the rest of the country (**Transvaal Highveld, Kruger Park**) rains come with sudden summer **thunderstorms**.

South Africa, however, is one of the world's drier countries: mean annual rainfall is 464

millimetres (18 inches), little more than half the global average. Only a third of the country gets enough rain for non-irrigated farming; just a quarter has perennial rivers, and often these are only seasonal.

COMPARATIVE CLIMATE CHART	JOHANNESBURG				DURBAN				CAPE TOWN			
	SUM JAN	AUT APR	WIN JULY	SPR OCT	SUM JAN	AUT APR	WIN JULY	SPR OCT	SUM JAN	AUT APR	WIN JULY	SPR OCT
MAX TEMP. °C	25	21	16	24	28	26	23	24	26	23	17	21
MIN TEMP. °C	15	11	5	12	21	17	10	17	16	12	7	10
MAX TEMP. °F	77	70	61	75	82	79	73	75	79	73	63	70
MIN TEMP. °F	59	52	41	54	70	63	50	63	61	54	45	50
HOURS SUN	8	8	9	9	6	7	7	5	11	7	6	9
RAINFALL in	5	2	0.5	3	5	3	2	4	1	2	3	2
RAINFALL mm	131	55	6	72	135	87	44	89	14	39	70	37

Plant Life

Vegetation is as varied as the climate, ranging from the hardy succulents, aloes and spring-flowering desert annuals of the parched western regions to the mountain evergreens and dense lowland bushveld of the Kruger National Park and Eastern Transvaal.

Much of the high plateau – the central and southern Transvaal and Orange Free State – consists of endless rolling grassland savannah which, because of the winter droughts and frosts, is mostly bare of trees. Only a tiny part of the country is covered by natural forests; these have been reduced by man to a scatter of relics, the largest being a magical strip of tall ironwoods and yellowwoods in the Knysna-Tsitsikamma area. Farther to the north, along Natal's balmy Indian Ocean shoreline, there are patches of evergreen subtropical trees, including raffia and ilala palms and, in the swampier coastal areas, mangroves.

> **SUNNY SOUTH AFRICA**
>
> South Africa has one of the world's most equitable climates; the average number of **cloudless hours** a day varies from **8** to **10** compared with New York's 7, Rome's 6 and London's modest 4. Some parts of the country – particularly in the dust-dry western region – record a bare 10 or so overcast days a year.

Wild Kingdom

South Africa's prime tourist attraction is without doubt its magnificent wildlife heritage, most impressive in the big-game areas of the Eastern Transvaal and Natal – areas well frequented by international visitors.

Sadly, the great herds and their predators have been crowded out by hunters, farmers and cattle ranchers and are now largely confined to proclaimed conservation areas. The largest and best known of these is the **Kruger National Park**, home to more varieties of wildlife than any other sanctuary in Africa, including the 'big five' and around 500 different kinds of birds.

Impressive, too, are the reserves of **Northern Natal** and **Zululand**, where dense vegetation provides ideal habitats for an astonishing array of animals and birds. Quite different in character but equally attractive to the adventurous visitor is the **Kalahari Gemsbok Park**, a vast wilderness of red dunes, dry riverbeds, sparse grasses and thornbush lying between Namibia and Botswana in the far north. If you want to do things in style, a number of exclusive private reserves and lodges, many located on the fringes of the Kruger Park, are in the superluxury class.

Conserving South Africa's Natural Heritage

South Africa's plant and animal habitats, like those elsewhere in Africa, are threatened – by urban sprawl, alien plant species, poachers, industry and mining, domestic cattle and the encroaching farmlands, and especially by the hunger of the rural peoples for water, firewood, grazing and living room.

Below: *Elephants foraging; a single adult consumes 300 kg (660 lb) of grass, shoots and stripped bark each day.*

But there is hope. Society's priorities are changing, and the voice of the conservationist is being heard much more clearly today. Moreover, those who make the decisions are starting to recognize that ecotourism can generate vast amounts of money. There is now a general conviction that the wellbeing of the wildlife and the interests of tourism need not conflict with the needs of rural Africans, and recent years have seen the appearance of 'multi-use' or 'resource' areas. These are integrated reserves – Natal's privately run, richly endowed Phinda reserve, for example – in which the people of the countryside, instead of being relocated, stay where they are and help conserve the environment. In return, they share in its resources, and benefit from tourism development – a win-win situation that holds real promise for the future.

SPOT THE BIG FIVE

Top of the game-viewing list are lion, elephant, rhino, buffalo and leopard. With luck and patience, all can be spotted in Kruger Park.
• The **leopard**, a shy, solitary creature, is a nocturnal hunter, and prefers to hide during the day. Its coat provides excellent camouflage.
• The **lion**, largest of Africa's carnivores, is also a nocturnal predator, but it can often be seen feeding on the remains of a kill in daylight.
• Herds of around 8,000 or more **elephant** roam in the Kruger, where individual bulls are renowned for the size of their tusks.
• The **buffalo** is regarded as one of the most dangerous and cunning of Africa's game species.
• The **white rhino**, despite its name, is dark in colour and is identified by its square-lipped mouth. The **black rhino** is recognized by its 'hooked' upper lip.

HISTORY IN BRIEF

Millennia ago, long before the arrival of the white man in southern Africa, bands of nomadic Bushman (or San) hunter-gatherers roamed the great spaces in search of sustenance and solitude. About 2,000 years ago some of the groups, having acquired sheep from the Sudanic peoples of the north, were introduced for the first time to the concept of property ownership and territory. Groups of these new, wealthier and more powerful San, known as the Khoikhoi (the Dutch called them Hottentots) migrated down the west coast. These were the first southern Africans to come into contact with the European seafarers of the 16th century.

Meanwhile, peoples of quite different cultures – Bantu-speakers who used iron and kept cattle – had occupied parts of what is now Zimbabwe in the far north, and around AD 1100 were migrating southwards and down along the east coast. By the 17th century the most powerful group, the Xhosa, had advanced as far as what is now the eastern Cape, and were on a direct collision course with the European colonists.

The Clash of Cultures

Although the Portuguese navigators (notably Dias and da Gama) pioneered the sea route to India in the years between 1488 and 1497, it was the Dutch who first

Above: *The lovely silver tree, largest of the extensive protea family.*

CAPE FLORAL KINGDOM

- The **Cape Floral Kingdom** is the smallest, but richest, of the world's six floral kingdoms.
- The vegetation type is known collectively as **fynbos** ('fine bush') and includes the lovely ericas (800 species) and proteas (the king protea is South Africa's national flower).
- More plant species occur on **Table Mountain** than are found in the entire British Isles.
- Many of the species are unique to the area, and are not found anywhere else in the world.
- Make a point of visiting **Kirstenbosch National Botanical Gardens**, which has a spectacular year-round display of indigenous flowering plants.

EARLY MAN

Southern and east Africa are regarded as the **'cradle of man'** – the regions where humankind's first ancestors appeared. The renowned archaeologist/palaeontologist **Raymond Dart** uncovered the first important hominid remains – a million-year-old infant skull – at **Taung**, in the northern Cape in 1924, naming the species *Australopithecus africanus*. Further finds by Dr Robert Broom in the western Transvaal's **Sterkfontein caves**, between 1936 and 1947, confirmed the long-debated link between ape-like creatures and early man.

established a permanent presence on the southern tip of Africa. In April 1652, Jan van Riebeeck and his small party arrived on the shores of the bay beneath Table Mountain to create a victualling station for the Dutch East India Company's passing fleets. Eventually, shortage of food prompted Van Riebeeck to release a number of Company officials from their employment contracts to set themselves up as farmers. He also imported slaves from other parts of Africa and from the Far East.

Both moves were significant. Having developed into a colony capable of growth, the Cape outpost expanded steadily over the following decades as 'trekboers' and farmers took their sheep and cattle and moved into the hinterland, pushing the Cape's boundaries ever outward. In the east they came up against the Xhosa, and competition for grazing land inevitably led to confrontation. In 1779 the first of nine bloody 'frontier wars' erupted.

Colonial Expansion

By the end of the century the power of the Netherlands was in decline, and in 1795 the British took over at the Cape. They withdrew for a brief period eight years later, returning in 1806 to rule the colony for the rest of the 19th century, during which white settlement expanded to cover the entire South African region. The story unfolded in three main areas of conflict.

In 1820 the colonial government, convinced that only large-scale immigration would bring stability to the **eastern Cape** region, brought in some 4,000 British settlers. For a time it seemed that borders could be agreed, and that the Xhosa would be left in peace, but eventually the settlers resumed their eastward push, and the black clans were progressively subdued.

Meanwhile the far eastern seaboard was also being colonized: British hunters and traders began to settle in **Port Natal** (now Durban) during the 1820s. Their arrival coincided with the *Difaqane*, a catastrophic series of forced marches triggered by the meteoric rise to power of the Zulu king **Shaka**: his newly fashioned army set out on a bloody war of conquest, igniting a chain reaction of violence and counterviolence that engulfed the entire east coast and much of the interior. During the 1830s, other whites rolled in from the west in their ox-wagons, **Boer (Afrikaner) trekkers** who came into conflict with Shaka's successor, Dingane, whom they finally defeated at Blood River in 1838. But it was the British who eventually prevailed – over both trekker and Zulu. The former were eased out of the fledgling colony of Natal in 1843; the latter, after a stunning victory at **Isandhlwana**, were crushed at **Ulundi** in 1879.

By the 1830s many Dutch-speaking Cape settlers, disenchanted with the British authorities at the Cape and incensed by the formal abolition of slavery in 1834 (which deprived the farmers of cheap labour), began to head into the interior in a mass migration known as the **Great Trek**.

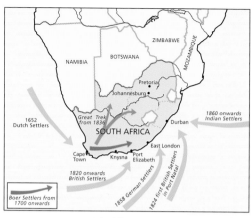

Colonial Migration

The exodus gathered momentum over the next few turbulent years, and eventually white people controlled much of the territory north of the Orange River. In the early 1850s their settlements were entrenched and strong enough to warrant the creation of two independent Boer republics: the **Orange Free State** and the **Transvaal**.

War and Union

The discovery of the fabulous **Kimberley** diamond fields at the end of the 1860s, and of the Witwatersrand's golden reef 25 years later, however, destroyed any chance of lasting peace between Boer and Briton. The northern region had become a prize worth competing for. Britain and the Transvaal fought it out on the slopes of **Majuba Hill** in Natal in 1881 (the Boers won) in a battle that left the former humiliated and the latter deeply suspicious of British imperial intentions. The two countries went to war again in 1899.

The Anglo-Boer conflict lasted nearly three years, reduced much of the northern countryside to a barren wilderness and left a legacy of bitterness.

But the British were determined on reconciliation. Their peace terms, set out in the **Treaty of Vereeniging** (1902), were generous to the defeated Afrikaners, and on 31 May 1910 the former Boer republics (Transvaal and

---

SHAKA: WARRIOR SUPREME

When Shaka succeeded to the Zulu chieftainship in 1816, the Zulu numbered just 1,500 people – but within a few years he was in control of the entire eastern (Natal) seaboard. The keys to this phenomenal expansion were the new weapons and fighting techniques he introduced to his army, among them:

• The **assegai**, a short stabbing spear that forced warriors into close combat (it replaced the throwing spear).
• The age-graded military system: **Zulu regiments** had their own living quarters, markings and regalia, and they fought as units. Regimental pride was a vital factor in battle.
• The famed Zulu battle formation (known as the **impi**), comprising the central 'chest' for frontal attack and the two 'horns' for encirclement.

Orange Free State) and the two British colonies (Cape and Natal) were united to become provinces of the new **Union of South Africa**. The country's first prime minister was Louis Botha, his deputy Jan Smuts, both Afrikaners of the 'enlightened' (pro-British) kind.

The black people had not been consulted in the creation of the unified state, and had practically no democratic rights within the new order.

Afrikanerdom Takes Over

The years between Union in 1910 and the crucial 1948 general election saw South Africa's transformation into a powerful, modern industrial nation. They were years of profound social change – and of a growing racial divide.

The legal separation of black and white – later known as **apartheid** – had always, even in the old 'liberal' Cape colony, been a part of the South African fabric. The Transvaal republic, for its part, had bluntly stated it would 'permit no equality between Coloured people and the white inhabitants, either in Church or State'. After Union, the racial gap widened.

The First World War (1914-18) stimulated industry and the growth of the urban areas. At the same time tens of thousands of people were being forced off the land – initially by cattle disease and the Anglo-Boer conflict, later by mechanization, always by drought. The blacks gathered around the cities in huge, strictly controlled locations, the 'poor whites' (mainly Afrikaners who could not compete with cheap African labour) on the fringes.

Conflict was inevitable. The economic depression heightened insecurity among the white wage-earners, and strikes and unrest became a regular feature of the between-wars years.

Below: *The Blood River Memorial commemorates the decisive 1838 battle between Zulu and Boer.*

In this tense climate, successive Union governments pushed through new racial measures ranging from job reservation and urban segregation to the formal allocation of land to confine the rural Africans. The moves, though, failed to satisfy the hardliners, a section of whom formed the extremist **Reunited National Party** in 1934 under the leadership of D.F. Malan, which steadily gained support among whites of both language groups (though especially among Afrikaners) during the next decade.

Jan Smuts, who led the country through the difficult years of the Second World War, badly underestimated this radical movement, and in 1948 Malan was elected to office by a slender majority to form South Africa's first all-Afrikaner government.

Above: *Pretoria's Union Buildings, a monument to Boer-Briton reconciliation in 1910.* **Below:** *The statue of Paul Kruger, 'father of Afrikanerdom', in Pretoria.*

The Apartheid Years

Although the nationalists of the 1950s and 1960s did not invent apartheid, they did tie together the existing threads of race prejudice to create one of the most all-embracing bodies of restrictive law ever devised.

The **Group Areas Act** (1950) segregated even further the country's cities and towns. Other laws involved racially based identity documents (the so-called **Pass Laws**), the classification of people according to colour, segregation of amenities ('whites-only' signs went up throughout the country) and the prohibition of mixed marriages and sex

across the colour line. It was Hendrik Verwoerd who, as Minister of Native Affairs (1950-58) and later as prime minister, contrived much of this, as well as the massively destructive Bantu Education Act condemning blacks to inferior schooling. He also laid the foundations of the homelands system – the **'Grand Apartheid'** design that carried segregation to its insane conclusion.

Verwoerd was assassinated in 1966, but his ruthless premiership had already seen South Africa's expulsion from the Commonwealth and its transition to a republic (1961).

STEPS TO FREEDOM

Among the high points of the liberation struggle in the early apartheid years were the award of the **Nobel Peace Prize** to **Albert Luthuli**, who became president of the African National Congress in 1952, and the signing of the **Freedom Charter** in 1955. The Charter, a crucial document that provided the framework of future protest, stated that South Africa belonged to all its people, black, brown and white, and went on to advocate:

- A nonracial democracy
- Equal rights and protection before the law
- Equal job and educational opportunities
- The redistribution of land and the nationalization of banks, mines and heavy industries.

The Liberation Movement

The black opposition, particularly the **African National Congress** (the ANC, South Africa's oldest political organization, was formed in 1912), had its roots in the disillusionment that set in after the Anglo-Boer War, a sense of betrayal reinforced by the exclusion of the black majority from the process leading up to Union in 1910.

The ANC remained committed to peaceful solutions for the next half century – a moderate stance which failed to advance the cause, and which, in 1959, prompted a breakaway by radical elements who formed the **Pan-Africanist Congress** (PAC). A year later, following the massacre at Sharpeville, both bodies were banned in terms of the Unlawful Organisations Act and went underground.

Soon afterwards the ANC launched its armed wing, **Umkhonto we Sizwe** (Spear of the Nation), and embarked on a wide-ranging programme of sabotage that led, in 1963, to the arrest of **Nelson Mandela** and other prominent Congress figures. In the following year, at the celebrated 'Rivonia trial', they were sentenced to life imprisonment and consigned to Robben Island, to the west of Cape Town's shores.

Protest and Reform

The Sharpeville massacre, where 69 demonstrators were gunned down by police, was the tragic culmination of a massive anti-Pass campaign launched by the PAC – led by **Robert Sobukwe** – and supported largely by youthful militants. **Sharpeville** was a crucial turning point in the country's affairs: before the incident, South Africa was still an accepted member of the community of nations; after March 1960 it faced isolation abroad and mounting race conflict at home.

Verwoerd's successors, **B.J. Vorster** (1966-78) and **P.W. Botha** (1978-90), tried hard to stem the tide – Vorster through a policy of 'detente' with independent black states, Botha through a programme of domestic reform. Botha's new tricameral constitution (1984) gave the Indian and so-called 'Coloured' communities a political voice (albeit a limited one) but Africans were yet again excluded from the central process, and the initiative was doomed from the start.

The seeds of failure, in fact, had been sown much earlier – in the 1970s, when the ideas of a talented activist named **Steve Biko** (he later died in custody) had taken root on university campuses and in the townships. Biko, founder of the radical 'black consciousness' movement, urged Africans to take pride in their self-sufficiency, in their colour and culture, and insisted that white people would be irrelevant in a 'post-Revolutionary South Africa'. Tensions came to a head when the use of Afrikaans as a teaching medium was enforced in black high schools. Powerful contributing factors, of course, were the denial of citizenship, general discrimination

Opposite: *Robben Island, onetime 'political' prison, counts Nelson Mandela as its most illustrious inmate.* **Below:** *Mandela and De Klerk, architects of the New South Africa.*

HISTORICAL CALENDAR

AD 200 First Bantu-speaking peoples enter South Africa; present basic pattern of black settlement established by the year 1500.

1497 Da Gama rounds Cape, charts sea route to India.

1652 Dutch settlers land at Cape, begin to colonize the interior; slaves imported.

1779 First of nine settler-Xhosa 'frontier wars' breaks out in eastern Cape.

1806 British occupy Cape to govern for remainder of century.

1824 White traders establish a community at Port Natal (now Durban).

1834 Slavery abolished.

1836-38 Great Trek begins as Boer (Afrikaner) families move into the interior.

1852-54 Transvaal and Orange Free State become independent Boer republics.

1869-70 Kimberley diamond fields discovered.

1886 Witwatersrand gold fields discovered; Johannesburg founded.

1899-1902 Anglo-Boer war; Boer guerillas resist fiercely but are eventually defeated.

1910 Unification of South Africa (Union).

1912 African National Congress founded.

1948 Afrikaner nationalists win election; apartheid era launched.

1960-61 Sharpeville massacre; South Africa leaves Commonwealth to become republic; liberation organizations banned.

1962 Nelson Mandela and others imprisoned 'for life'.

1976 Soweto students revolt; disturbances spread.

1991-93 F.W. de Klerk replaces P.W. Botha as president; Mandela released; democracy talks held.

1994 Democratic elections; Mandela inaugurated as president on 10 May.

LEADING LIGHTS

In 1993 two South Africans shared the Nobel Peace Prize for their part in launching the country on the path to democracy:

Nelson Rolihlahla Mandela, born 1918; qualified as lawyer 1942; banned under Suppression of Communism Act 1952; helped found ANC military wing 1961; arrested for conspiring to promote sabotage and insurrection 1963; imprisoned 1964; released 1990.

Frederick Willem de Klerk, born 1936; active in student politics; qualified as lawyer; elected leader of Transvaal National Party and known as hardline conservative until 1989 when, as state president, introduced far-reaching political reforms.

and lack of civic facilities. On 16 June 1976, some 10,000 young students staged a protest march through the dusty streets of the townships and then battled it out with the security forces. The date is now commemorated as **Soweto Day**. The riots, and the troubled years that followed, established a pattern: of unrest designed to 'make the country ungovernable' and of tough police reaction. By the late 1980s the townships were in a state of anarchy, and even conservative whites realized that they could no longer hold onto power.

The New Era

In 1989 the ailing P.W. Botha was ousted in favour of **F.W. De Klerk**, a politician not noted for his liberal views but a pragmatist nevertheless. The changes that followed were rapid, fundamental, and dramatic. On 2 February 1990, at the opening session of parliament, De Klerk announced the unbanning of the ANC, the South African Communist Party, the PAC and other organizations. Two weeks later Nelson Mandela, behind bars for the past 27 years, walked to freedom.

The decades of white political supremacy had finally come to an end; the new South Africa was about to be born.

GOVERNMENT AND ECONOMY

A new system of government; the future direction of the economy; redistribution of wealth; in fact, the entire restructuring of society – these were the issues fundamental to the negotiation process that began in 1991. Discussions over the next three years were complex and plagued by setbacks, and by a political arena that was fraught with violence.

Above: *Durban's harbour is the country's foremost seaport; it is also among the biggest and busiest in the southern hemisphere.*

By the beginning of 1994, however, the protagonists – the leaders of more than 20 political parties meeting at the World Trade Centre near Johannesburg – had reached agreement, and the route to a new democratic dispensation had been charted.

Key elements of the concord were an **interim constitution**, which made provision for a **government of national unity**, a **National Assembly** of 400 members elected by universal suffrage, and for a federal framework encompassing nine **provincial assemblies**. During its five-year life the National Assembly, working within a predetermined formula, would produce a **final constitution** and a comprehensive **Bill of Rights**.

One-person, one-vote elections, held at the end of April 1994, gave the African National Congress a 62 per cent majority in the National Assembly, clear majorities in six of the provincial legislatures and a slender majority in the seventh. Chief Mangosuthu Buthelezi's Inkatha Freedom Party won the KwaZulu Natal province, F.W. De Klerk's Nationalists the Western Cape.

On 10 May, in the amphitheatre of Pretoria's historic Union Buildings, and to an audience of foreign dignitaries numbering more than have been seen together at any

SOUTH AFRICA'S FOREIGN EARNINGS	
Precious metals (gold, platinum, etc.)	**39%**
Base metals and articles thereof	**14%**
Minerals	**11%**
Vehicles and machinery (including transport equipment)	**6%**
Chemicals	**5%**
Agricultural products (animals, vegetables, fruit, fats and oils)	**5%**
Pulp, paper, products	**3%**
Textiles, clothing and footwear	**3%**
Prepared foodstuffs (including tobacco)	**3%**
Wood, leather and their products	**1%**
Rubber, plastic and their products	**1%**
Other (including scientific equipment)	**9%**

event since John F. Kennedy's funeral in 1963, Nelson Mandela was inaugurated as the first president of a fully democratic South Africa. A crowd of 150 000 watched the event on a giant screen from just outside the buildings.

Wealth and Poverty

South Africa is a curious mix of First World sophistication and Third World underdevelopment. On the one hand it has immense natural resources, employs the latest technologies, supports advanced industrial and commercial structures, and there is a lot of money at the top end of the economic scale. On the other hand, standards of education among the majority of black South Africans are low; there are too few jobs and services for the rapidly expanding population and the 'poverty cycle', if not quite so horrific as it is in some other African countries, is very real, threatening stability and confusing the decision-making process.

What most people are agreed upon, is that South Africa's wealth will have to be divided more equitably, the gap between rich and poor narrowed. Whether this is achieved through a socialist-type command economy, or through the free play of market forces or, most likely, something in between, has yet to be decided.

The contributions to South Africa's economic wellbeing take no account of the dynamic 'informal economy' that is flourishing and which is partly a product of serious unemployment. The term covers home-based businesses, market trading, hawking, minibus services, crafts and *shebeens* (bars) – a kaleidoscope of mostly tiny ventures which are thought to account for around 30% of total domestic income.

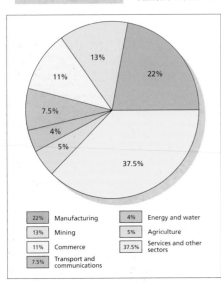

22%	Manufacturing	4%	Energy and water
13%	Mining	5%	Agriculture
11%	Commerce	37.5%	Services and other sectors
7.5%	Transport and communications		

Leading Economic Sectors

These small enterprises have a vital part to play: they provide much-needed work, generate wealth, develop skills and entrepreneurial expertise – and they are helping pioneer the economic future.

Infrastructure

South Africa has an excellent road network that covers the entire country.

Transnet, the nation's semiprivate rail undertaking, operates diesel and electric locomotives, carrying 800 million passengers and 200 million tonnes (220,5 million tons) of goods a year. Travel of the most luxurious kind can be enjoyed on the famed **Blue Train**, which plies between Pretoria/Johannesburg and Cape Town, and which has now extended its service to the beautiful Eastern Transvaal.

The main harbours are at Durban, Cape Town (Table Bay), Port Elizabeth, Richards Bay, East London (the only river port) and Saldanha Bay. Cargo handling is highly mechanized, storage sophisticated; the bigger outlets have pre-cooling facilities, grain elevators, in-transit warehouses and container terminals.

AFRICA'S ECONOMIC SUPERPOWER

South Africa is the engine room of sub-Saharan Africa. Home to just one-twentieth of the continent's total population, it accounts for:

40% of Africa's industrial output
25% of the gross continental product
65% of electricity generated
45% of mineral production
40% of the maize harvest (in normal years)
66% of steel output

South Africans drive nearly half of Africa's motor vehicles and use over a third of its telephones.

Below: *Sasolburg's refinery: the world's only viable large-scale oil-from-coal enterprise.*

South African Airways, the national carrier, operates a fleet of Boeing 747 airliners over a network that spans the globe, and domestic services that cover the main centres. Private airlines serve major, and smaller, towns. There are international airports between Johannesburg and Pretoria, and one each in Durban and Cape Town.

Industry

The country's natural resources, added to a vast pool of labour (although this is expensive by the standards of developed countries – productivity is low), technical expertise and political necessity have led South Africa towards industrial self-sufficiency. But the cost has been high: protective tariffs have cushioned locally made goods, pushing up domestic prices and making it hard for companies to compete on world markets.

The largest manufacturing sectors are metal products (steel, and everything from cranes and mills to specialized machinery and computer parts); nonmetallic mineral products, vehicles and transport equipment, chemicals and pharmaceuticals, processed foods, clothing and textiles.

Energy

Eskom, the country's electricity supply utility, produces over 60% of all power generated on the African continent. Coal is the main source, though Eskom also operates two

hydro-electric power, two pump-storage, three gas-turbine power stations and one nuclear plant (at Koeberg, near Cape Town). However, millions of people – in townships as well as the rural areas – are without power, relying on wood and paraffin for cooking and heating.

Left: *Molten gold is poured at the President Brand mine in the Orange Free State.*

Eskom is giving priority to their needs, and has plans to bring electricity to every household in the country. Some of South Africa's fuel requirements are met by three huge oil-from-coal plants and by oil and gas from the newly discovered fields off the southern coast.

Social Services

In the early 1990s housing, health and education were in crisis. Around 45% of the population exist 'below minimum living levels'; 2·3 million are in urgent need of nutritional support; 72 children die of malnutrition each day. In 1993 the housing shortfall was estimated at over 1·5 million units and growing by the month as thousands left the countryside for the towns.

THE PEOPLE

More than a third of South Africa's population of **39 million** lives in and around the cities and towns. And sprawling untidily around these, in turn, are what used to be called 'African' townships, many of which started life as 'locations' for cheap and temporary labour – makeshift, soulless places in the early days, virtually devoid of civic amenities. **Soweto**, close to Johannesburg, is the best known.

However, urban conditions are improving – the more permanent areas, though grossly overcrowded, have their basic services, electricity, schools, clinics, community centres, sports fields, clubs and shebeens. In some places the streets are paved, and there are pockets of substantial and sometimes – notably in Soweto – palatial houses for the rapidly emerging African middle class.

But development can't keep pace with the numbers of people driven from a countryside no longer able to support them, and who are lured to the towns by the prospect

MINING

The country has the world's largest known deposits of **gold** (51% of global reserves), **platinum**-group metals (71%), high-grade **chromium** (55%), **manganese** which is vital to the steel industry (78%), **vanadium**, **fluorspar** and **andalusite**, plus massive deposits of **diamonds**, **iron ore**, **coal** (58 billion tons of proven reserves), **uranium**, **nickel** and **phosphates** – nearly 60 commodities in all.

Around 600 tons of gold a year – 40% of the world's total output – is extracted from the mines of the East and West Rand to either side of Johannesburg, and on the giant Free State fields around Welkom.

Below: *At the rock face, drilling the golden seam 2,000 m (6,560 ft) below ground. South Africa's mines are among the world's deepest.*

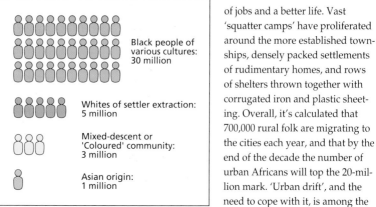

Black people of various cultures: 30 million

Whites of settler extraction: 5 million

Mixed-descent or 'Coloured' community: 3 million

Asian origin: 1 million

South Africa's Population

of jobs and a better life. Vast 'squatter camps' have proliferated around the more established townships, densely packed settlements of rudimentary homes, and rows of shelters thrown together with corrugated iron and plastic sheeting. Overall, it's calculated that 700,000 rural folk are migrating to the cities each year, and that by the end of the decade the number of urban Africans will top the 20-million mark. 'Urban drift', and the need to cope with it, is among the country's most pressing problems.

Language

South Africa's cultural mix is reflected in its confusing variety of languages and dialects. **English** and **Afrikaans** have been the official languages in the past, though English is likely to become the more favoured. Afrikaans, which stems from the High Dutch of the early settlers, is the mother tongue of the Afrikaner people, and of most of the so-called 'Coloureds', though many others, both black and white, use it as a second language.

Religion

Religion is determined largely by cultural origin. Biggest of the **Christian** groups are the Dutch Reformed churches, which have Calvinist roots, followed by the Roman Catholic, Methodist, Anglican, Presbyterian and Baptist congregations.

Around 120,000 South Africans adhere to the **Judaic** faith. **Hindus** number nearly 600,000 and **Moslems** 400,000, both concentrated in Natal, although a large number in the Cape also follow Islam.

Combining Christianity with elements of traditional belief are over 2,000 indigenous, independent churches, most of them in the Transvaal. Biggest is the Zion Christian Church, which has its own 'city' near

---

SPEAKING IN MANY TONGUES

No less than **eight languages** in South Africa are each spoken by more than one million people (of a total population of 39 million). Understandable, then, is the difficulty in establishing which ones to give equal merit. Based on first, or home language, status the most commonly spoken ones are:

Zulu	22%
Xhosa	17%
Afrikaans	15%
North Sotho	10%
English	9%
Tswana	9%
South Sotho	7%
Tsonga	4%
Swazi	3%
Ndebele	2%
Venda	2%

Source: Professor G.K. Schuring, HSRC, 1991

Left: A herbalist with the myriad and mysterious ingredients of his trade.

Pietersburg in the far north. Most of the groups believe in prophet-healers, and some wear brightly coloured uniforms and robes.

African traditional beliefs – still influential, even among mainstream Christians – are based on a Supreme Being who is infinitely remote from humankind. Ancestors provide the link between the living and the dead, and are therefore placated and respected. Lower in the rank is the Inkosi Phezulu – king or paramount chief – and after him, the headman. Last in the hierarchy are ordinary men, women, and children.

> ### TRADITIONAL HEALERS
>
> Diviners, or spirit mediums, play a significant role in traditional cultures. Known to the Zulu as **sangomas**, they are recruited by the ancestors, undergo a rigorous apprenticeship, and act as intermediaries between the living and their forefathers. Techniques vary but, generally, practitioners can predict, divine and heal a multitude of ills, usually of the psychological or social kind.
>
> More down to earth is the **herbalist**, who has filled the role of doctor in traditional village society for centuries, and whose prime function is to cure physical ailments. He (or she) is able to prescribe from a wide range of herbs, tree-bark and other medicinal flora of the veld, many of which are known to have valuable curative properties.

Traditional Cultures

Middle-class South African lifestyles, certainly in the towns and their more upmarket suburbs, are virtually indistinguishable from those of any American or European city. Pockets of exotic culture do, however, flourish here and there, and something of the old Africa still survives in the country areas.

Indian society   The country's Asian community, 85% of which lives in and around Greater Durban on the east coast, is a mostly prosperous one that retains the distinctive customs and convictions of the Indian mainland. Lifestyles, certainly among the older generation, are underpinned by the *kutum* – the patriarchal, disciplined extended family that regulates relationships and social interaction. Indian society is strongly unified, but also organized according to the Hindu or Moslem faith, each of which has its own strict rules that modify behaviour, manners, food and drink.

The Cape's Islamic community   Adhering to the Islamic faith are the Cape Malays, brought into the country in the late 1600s as slaves from Ceylon, and from the

The country is renowned for its ethnic melting pot of cultures and creeds. Here, four of South Africa's many faces. **Clockwise from top left:** *Mixed-descent Capetonian; sari-clad Natal Indian; rural Zulu; Afrikaner farmer.*

Indonesian islands of Java, Sumatra and Bali. Some were political prisoners, others high-ranking exiles, and many were skilled craftsmen who, among other things, added decorative charm to early South African architecture. This is a devout, integrated society of around 200,000, which has evolved its own distinctive cuisine and cultural traditions.

Tribal life European settlement, the drift to the cities and the influence of western culture has destroyed much of the old order, but fragments of traditional Africa do still survive today.

Some **Ndebele** village women still wear heavy anklets and necklaces that can never be removed, and paint the walls of their homesteads in vividly coloured geometric patterns. The **Swazi** of the Eastern Transvaal celebrate unity and the rebirth of their chiefs in a zestful, week-

long marathon of dance, song, rituals and endurance tests. **Venda** girls perform the domba snake-dance to mark their entry into womanhood. **Xhosa** women are famed for their beadwork (the various patterns represent status as well as clan identity), and young Xhosa country boys still go through a long and painful initiation ritual.

Drive through the byways of Natal and you may see beehive huts made by **Zulu** craftsmen with an eye for beauty as well as tradition. Here, too, are beaded head-dresses and the ceremonial regalia of a vanished and perhaps prouder age.

The visual remnants of ancient Africa are everywhere, though it is disappearing fast and much of it is especially laid on for the tourist. More resistant to time are the abstracts – folklore, etiquette and taboo, religion, heredi-tary rank and the bonds of kinship, concepts of property and land ownership, the nature and obligations of betrothal and marriage. In tribal life, marriages are still arranged by the family and the bride-price, or *lobolo*, is often paid in cows and oxen (the custom is still observed among city dwellers, though hard cash has replaced live-stock as the appropriate currency).

Sounds of Africa

The African people are renowned for their natural gift for rhythm, harmony and spontaneous song. Zulu musi-cal instruments are few and simple – a double-ended cowhide drum, a rattle worn on the ankle or shaken by hand, a reed pipe. But there is also the powerful, deep-throated roar of men's voices in part harmony, the keen-ing descant of the women, the clapping of hands and the stamping of feet. Other groups create music using xylo-phones, marimbas and several types of stringed instru-ment originating from the shooting bow, some with gourds attached to the bow-string for resonance.

Sport and Recreation

South Africa's wonderfully sunny climate is perfect for outdoor life; its people are enthusiastic and, many of them, accomplished sportspersons.

TOWNSHIP JIVE

With the movement to the cities, a new and distinctive sound has emerged. Called **Mbaqanga**, it draws much from the original music of Africa, but has been influ-enced by American big-band jazz and soul, giving it a vibrant character of its own. Township music defies any simple definition – there are too many ingredients, too many roots – but unmistak-able is the throbbing under-tone of pure Africa.

Mbaqanga is the African word for maize bread and, like the food it describes, it feeds a deep hunger.

Below: *Marimba player at Cape Town's Baxter Theatre: ancient instruments feature in much of modern South African music.*

Soccer is king within the African communities, which support around 15,000 clubs and produce nearly a million regular players. Among the leading professional clubs are Kaizer Chiefs, Orlando Pirates, Mamelodi Sundowns, Jomo Cosmos and Moroka Swallows (all in the Johannesburg–Pretoria area) and AmaZulu in Natal. Track athletics and, especially, long-distance road-running are also gaining a large following; world-class runners have already emerged.

Rugby is almost an obsession among Afrikaners, and until the early 1980s, Springbok sides often reigned as unofficial world champions. Both Afrikaans- and English-speaking whites are passionate about cricket which, as the result of an imaginative development programme, is becoming increasingly popular among people of colour.

Hiking, jogging and cycling have a huge number of devotees. South Africa's more than 400 golf clubs welcome visitors, green fees are reasonable, and most courses are immaculately maintained. Bowling and tennis clubs are equally welcoming.

Food and Drink

Special culinary drawcards are the local meat and venison (including springbok, ostrich and occasionally warthog), fruit, fish, shellfish – particularly rock lobster

Below: *Johannesburg's giant Ellis Park stadium, venue for international rugby and much else.*

SUNNY SKIES AND BRAAIVLEIS

The **'braai'**, one of South Africa's more lasting traditions, is a barbecue featuring well-marinated meats, and spicy **boerewors** ('farmer's sausage'). Accompanied by beer and bonhomie, few visitors escape an invitation to one. Summer's sunny climate is perfect for these gatherings, and on weekends tantalizing aromas of sizzling meat fill the air across suburbia.

(crayfish) and abalone (perlemoen). There isn't, however, a single, coherent South African philosophy of food – the country is too ethnically diverse, and eating patterns are drawn from many different parts of the world.

Nevertheless, the eating traditions of some of the immigrant groups – Greek, German, Portuguese, for example – are more prominent than others in various regions. Durban restaurants are renowned for their fiery curries, *tandoori* meats and marvellous *breyanis*; the Cape for traditional fare in which Karoo lamb, venison (particularly springbok pie), sweet potato, cinnamon-flavoured pumpkin and stickily sweet *konfyt* are popular.

The Cape, too, is the home of 'Malay' cooking, noted for its fragrant *bredies* (a mutton stew with potato, onion and vegetables), its lightly spiced *boboties* and luscious desserts. The cuisine's origins are mainly Indonesian, though over the centuries other culinary traditions have been influential: curries and samoosas from India; puddings, tarts and biscuits from the early Dutch settlers; the sweet preserves of the French Huguenots.

Also part of the South African experience is *potjiekos*, a long-simmering stew created with layers of meat, potatoes and a variety of vegetables in a large cast-iron pot, cooked over an open fire to allow the flavours to mingle.

Traditional African cooking does not appear on many menus. The ordinary meal of the day in townships and villages is usually a no-nonsense affair of maize meal ('samp'), vegetables and, less often, stewed meat. For most of the indigenous people, eating remains a practical and often formidably challenging necessity.

South African wines, both red and white, are generally very good. Some of the labels are fast gaining a reputation for excellence, a generous handful are quite sublime, and many are receiving accolades in international competitions. The wines are still fairly cheap by international standards, though prices have been rising. Some handy and informative volumes on the country's wines can be found in most bookshops.

2
Johannesburg and Pretoria

Johannesburg, South Africa's largest metropolis, and Pretoria, the country's administrative capital, are located 56 kilometres (35 miles) apart on the highest part of the great interior plateau known as the Highveld. Johannesburg was founded on gold, discovered in 1886 by George Harrison, an itinerant Australian prospector, on the **Witwatersrand** that has yielded the world's richest deposits of the metal.

Pretoria, to the north, is very different in character: older, more sedate, it lies in the warm and fertile valley of the Apies (little ape) River, its eastern suburbs hugging the lovely **Magaliesberg** range of hills, the central area overlooked by Meintjieskop and the imposing façade of the government's Union Buildings.

To the south of Johannesburg lies the enormous 'black' urban conglomerate of **Soweto**. Further south is another concentration of industrial towns known as the **Vaal Triangle**. Together, Pretoria, the Witwatersrand and the Vaal Triangle – the PWV region – are South Africa's economic heartland.

JOHANNESBURG

Johannesburg has few claims to beauty, though it does have its belt of greenery along the banks of the **Braamfonteinspruit**, and its tree-garlanded golf courses and leafy northern suburbs. To the south, old mine dumps litter the landscape, and the central area is a modern concrete-and-glass jungle of high-rises and congested streets, where the primary preoccupation is with busi-

CLIMATE

The Transvaal Highveld has one of the world's most agreeable climates: **summer** days tend to be **warm** and **windless**. Although **winter** days are sunny, crisp and invigorating, **nights** are often bitter with **frost**. This is a summer rainfall region, and from Dec to Feb, late-afternoon downpours are common. Both Pretoria and Johannesburg enjoy an average of nine hours' sunshine a day.

Opposite: *Although Johannesburg's mines have moved out, the city's old workings remain, quietly rusting away in the sun.*

DON'T MISS

*** The Lost City and
Sun City
*** A trip on the Blue Train
*** Gold Reef City
** A tour of Soweto
** Game-viewing at the
Pilanesberg National Park
** An evening at Carousel
Entertainment World.

ness. But the city as a whole has its attractions: excellent hotels and restaurants, shopping malls, galleries, museums, theatres – and a vibrancy, an uninhibited zest for life that is reflected on the social as well as the business scene. The heart of Johannesburg is in many ways a microcosm of the country; a cultural kaleidoscope of past and future: postmodern towers are juxtaposed with a few stately survivors of the city's gold-rush days, and pockets of established Portuguese, Indian and Chinese traders jostle with newer African *muti* shops and pavement vendors. Street crime is at least as prevalent as it is in other big cities of the world, making walking, especially on your own after dark, a risky option. Guided tours are the best way of experiencing the inner city's charisma.

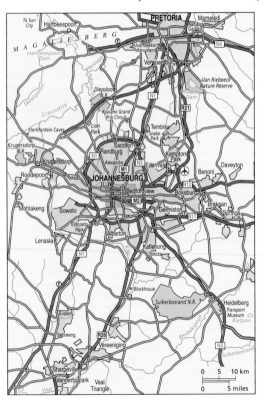

City Sightseeing

A good place from which to get your bearings is **Carlton Panorama**, the observation deck on the 50th floor of the Carlton Centre (Johannesburg's highest building) in Commissioner Street. Also on offer here are a gold exhibition and two sound-and-light shows. It's open from 09:00 to 23:00. Don't miss **Diagonal Street** with its gleaming skyscrapers, one of which houses the **Stock Exchange** (to enquire about free weekday tours, tel: (011) 833-6580).

Shops and clubs are open day and night in the cosmopolitan, densely populated flatland of **Hillbrow**.

Market Theatre Complex ★★

Situated at Mary Fitzgerald Square, this lively complex has four auditoriums, an Indian fruit market, a flower market, clothing and jewellery boutiques, an outstanding second-hand bookshop, bistros – among them legendary **Kippie's Jazz Bar**, designed on the lines of a Victorian public toilet – and live experimental theatre that draws on the African experience.

Gold Reef City ★★★

An evocative reconstruction of pioneer Johannesburg, Gold Reef City is located on the old **Crown Mines** site, six kilometres (four miles) south of central Johannesburg. The Crown produced 1·4 million kilograms (3·1 million pounds) of gold – worth about US$20 billion at current prices – in its long, honourable lifetime; visitors can descend a mineshaft to explore the underground workings, and watch gold being poured.

Other attractions are displays of traditional dancing; tram and horse-drawn omnibus rides; a Victorian funfair, pub and tea parlour; replicas of an early theatre, stock exchange, newspaper office; house museums furnished in period style; and many attractive speciality shops (diamonds, leatherware, pottery, glassware, lace, coins,

CITY OF GOLD

Only mountainous dumps and the rusting headgear of the gold mines survive as a reminder of the heady days when Johannesburg (known to the Zulus as eGoli, or city of gold) was more of a diggers' camp than a city. The industry has moved outwards, to exploit the still-immense wealth of the East and West Rand, and the giant Orange Free State fields. Visits can be arranged through the Chamber of Mines, tel: (011) 838-8211. South Africa's gold output accounts for 35% of the global total. Vaal Reefs is the world's biggest mine; Western Deep Levels holds the world's depth record.

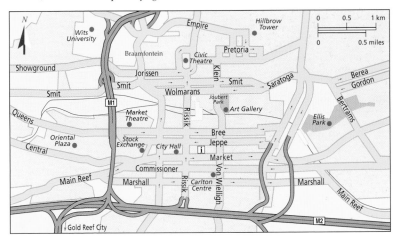

OPEN-AIR MARKETS

Regular open-air craft markets are:
Johannesburg flea market, every Sat in front of the Market Theatre; the **Village Flea Market** in Hillbrow, every Sat and Sun; **Petticoat Lane** in Witkoppen (Victorian gazebo-like stalls in a lake setting, farmyard animals), Fri 15:00-21:00, every Sat and Sun; **Organic Village Market** in Bryanston (cottage industries, natural-fibre clothing, organically grown vegetables, fruits and spices), Thu and Sat, 09:00-13:00. Over the first weekend in each month you can visit **Sandton Collectables** in the Parkview Shopping Centre, and **Artists' Market** at Zoo Lake, an art-and-craft expo; the 700-stall **People's Show** is held every Sat at the National Exhibition Centre near the Crown Mines site.

stamps, curios). The **Crown Restaurant** serves gourmet fare; the period-style **Gold Reef City Hotel** offers accommodation from the standard to the luxurious.

Gold Reef City Helicopters will take you on bird's-eye viewing trips of Johannesburg and Soweto, lasting seven minutes (Saturday and Sunday from 11:30).

Pick of the Museums and Galleries

Africana Museum, adjacent to the Market Theatre: explores the culture and history of southern Africa.

Planetarium in Braamfontein: houses the wonders of star travel in armchair comfort, including time travel back to the age of the pyramids, Stonehenge and so on. Multivisual sky shows are held Friday to Sunday.

Transnet Museum on the Old Station concourse in De Villiers Street: covers the whole public-transport scene from steam railways to airways and harbours.

Klein Jukskei Motor Museum in Randburg: has an impressive collection of early and rare vehicles.

Johannesburg Art Gallery in Joubert Park, central Johannesburg: offers impressive permanent and interesting temporary exhibitions, which include South African, English, French and Dutch works.

Wits Art Gallery in Senate House, Jorissen Street, Braamfontein: displays the Standard Bank collection of African Art; open Tuesday to Friday, 10:00 to 16:00.

Kim Sacks Art Gallery in Bellevue: highlights tribal and folk art; for opening times, tel: (011) 648-6107.

Everard Read Contemporary Gallery, housed in a controversial building in Rosebank: showcase for mainly up-and-coming young artists and wildlife art.

Top Theatres

The **Civic Theatre** in Braamfontein is a 1,120-seat venue for drama, opera, ballet, light musical productions, orchestral concerts, recitals and marionette shows; the small **Arena** in Rosebank is often used by the Performing Arts Council (PACT) for innovative productions; the **Market Theatre** in the city centre (*see* p. 33) presents theatre that caters to all tastes, from 'ethnic' and experimental shows to drawing-room comedy; the **Johannesburg City Hall** is a venue for orchestral concerts and other shows (programmes obtainable at the Publicity Association); the **Linder Auditorium** at the Johannesburg College of Education presents symphony concerts; and the **Standard Bank Arena** in Doornfontein is the venue for large-scale concerts and indoor tennis competitions.

Shopping

'World in one' outlets (restaurants, cinemas, banks, sophisticated shops): **Carlton Centre** and **Smal Street pedestrian mall**, central city; in the northern suburbs: **Rosebank Mall** and nearby **The Firs**, Rosebank; **Eastgate**, Broadway Extension; **Hyde Park Corner**, Jan

PLANTS AND ANIMALS OF THE CONCRETE JUNGLE

For a breath of fresh air, pay a visit to:
** **Florence Bloom Bird Sanctuary** in Delta Park: large variety of species, natural-history museum, two small dams with hides.
** **Johannesburg Zoo** in Parkview: more than 3,000 kinds of animal, bird and reptile; for tours, tel: (011) 646-2000.
** **Johannesburg Botanical Gardens** in Emmarentia: lovely rose and herb gardens.
** **Lion Park** north of the city, on the old Pretoria-Krugersdorp Road: 1-km (half a mile) driving trail.
* **Lipizzaner stallions** at Kyalami on Sun: book through Computicket.
* **Melrose Bird Sanctuary** in Melrose.
* **Snake Park** at Halfway House in Midrand.

Opposite page: *Gold Reef City ranks among Johannesburg's leading tourist attractions.* **Left:** *African artefacts on sale outside the Market Theatre.*

Above: *A fascinating Johannesburg shop selling traditional African herbal and other medicines.*

Opposite: *Standard housing in Soweto, although an increasing number of homes are decidedly impressive.*

BLACK TAXIS

From the late 1980s onward, black taxis have rapidly become a major business concern. Today's minibuses are mainly Japanese: the Toyota Hi-Aces are known as '**Zola Budds**' because they're fast; at one time the slower Isuzus were named '**Mary Deckers**', but the term has since fallen away. Plying the highways in their thousands, these taxis are cheap, fast and sociable, but their safety record is not reassuring.

Smuts Avenue; **Sandton City** in Sandton; new **Fourways Mall** (one of the largest in the country) in Fourways. Smaller outlets cater especially for the visitor, offering African craft work, curios, hides, local pottery and so forth; ask the Publicity Association for guidance.

Daily markets: **Diagonal Street**, near the stock exchange (stores sell African blankets through witchdoctors' herbs and bones); **African Market** in the Atrium Centre, Sandton; the **Oriental Plaza** in Fordsburg (an Indian market comprising 275 shops, a must for bargain-hunters). At **Fisherman's Village** on Bruma Lake in Bedfordview are cosmopolitan eating places and boutiques on cobbled, flower-bedecked streets.

Soweto

South Africa's best-known 'black' city (though the demise of apartheid has rendered the term obsolete) straggles across nearly 100 square kilometres (39 square miles) of dusty and unkempt terrain to the southwest of Johannesburg. Much of it is electrified, a growing number of its streets are paved, and the more prosperous residents have large and attractive homes. However, formal development has been haphazard and slow, and the majority of Sowetans live in so-called matchbox houses in overcrowded conditions (there are no high-rises).

Soweto – an acronym of SOuth WEstern TOwnships – was originally designed as a dormitory town. Many workers still commute daily by train and minibus to Johannesburg and other nearby centres. Big business has passed Soweto by (until recently it was forced to do so by law), and commercial activity is represented by about 4,000 tiny 'spaza' stores and by the burgeoning 'informal sector' (hawking, markets, backyard industries).

Soweto has few of the civic amenities (parks, public libraries) that city dwellers of the more advanced countries take for granted. The local hospital, **Baragwanath**, is Africa's largest, while *The Sowetan* newspaper is the country's fastest growing in circulation terms. Social life revolves around the football stadiums and grounds, the myriad *shebeens* (home bars) and the more upmarket nightclubs and community halls.

Visits are arranged by the **Carlton Hotel** (coaches leave from outside the building); and by **Jimmy's Face to Face Tours** (scheduled excursions depart from outside selected hotels in Sandton, Rosebank and central Johannesburg).

SATELLITE CITIES

Greater Soweto is by no means the region's only 'black' area: the Witwatersrand is ringed by sprawling townships, at least seven of which are home to more than 100,000 residents each. Part of the Witwatersrand are **Alexandra** (124,500) to the north of Johannesburg; **Tembisa** (209,000) in the northeast; **Daveyton** (151,000) to the east; and to the south, **Tokoza** and **Katlehong** (201,000). South of the Rand the satellites of Vanderbijlpark – **Sharpeville, Boipatong** and **Bophelong** – jointly house some 143,000 people. **Mamelodi** (154,845) is Pretoria's largest black satellite.

BEAUTIFUL BUREAUCRACY

The splendid crescent-shaped complex of the **Union Buildings**, South Africa's bureaucratic heartland, sits on a hill known as Meintjieskop, from which there are good views of the city and countryside. The neoclassical buildings, conceived by the renowned British architect Herbert Baker, were completed in 1913 and later served as the model for the larger seat of the Raj government in New Delhi. The beautifully landscaped grounds are open to the public. Among features of note are the **amphitheatre**; the **Garden of Remembrance**; and the **Delville Wood** memorial, commemorating the S.A. Brigade's heroism in the mud of Flanders in July 1916.

THE BLUE TRAIN

The famed Blue Train offers the ultimate in luxury travel. The handsome, 16-coach, 107-berth train leaves from Pretoria station, stopping at Johannesburg before heading for Cape Town. Passengers can watch some of the country's most spectacular scenery glide by from the elegantly appointed dining car where gourmet meals are served. For further information, tel: (012) 315-2436.

PRETORIA

Base and symbol of the country's administration, this South African city bears the name best known to foreign tourists. Pretoria is a handsome city, noted for its stately and (some of them) historic buildings, for its parks and gardens, its splendid wealth of indigenous flora and for its jacarandas. Some 80,000 of these exquisite trees grace the open areas and line about 650 kilometres (400 miles) of well-laid-out streets. Pretoria's informal name – the '**Jacaranda City**' – derives from their lilac-blossomed glory in springtime (October).

In its administrative capacity, Pretoria hosts many a foreign embassy, as well as the top brass of the country's military, but it has its fair share of industry too. Originally based on the giant Iscor steelworks just to the southwest, its industrial sector includes engineering and food processing and, mainly at nearby Cullinan, diamond mining (the 3,106-carat Cullinan Diamond – the biggest ever found – was unearthed at the town's Premier Mine in 1905).

The city is also a centre of research and learning. Within and around its limits are Pretoria University; Unisa, the world's largest correspondence university; Onderstepoort, an internationally renowned veterinary research institute; the Medical University of South Africa (Medunsa); the Council for Scientific and Industrial Research (CSIR); the Human Sciences Research Council (HSRC); and the SA Bureau of Standards (SABS).

Church Square ★

Pretoria became the capital of the independent Boer (Afrikaner) republic of the Transvaal in 1860 and grew up, quite gracefully, around Church Square, the original marketplace and focal point of the isolated Boer community's *nagmaal* (communion), baptisms and weddings. Among the more prominent buildings here are the **Old Raadsaal** (parliament), built in French Renaissance style and completed in 1889, and the graceful **Palace of Justice**. The square's northern frontage is vaguely reminiscent of the Place de la Concorde in Paris, its southern of London's Trafalgar Square (though of course these two places are much grander), and its most striking feature is Dutch sculptor Anton van Wouw's bronze statue of **Paul Kruger**, 'Father of Afrikanerdom'.

State Theatre ★★

On its completion in 1981, this complex comprising five theatres and a public square was the largest of its kind in the southern hemisphere. Art works created by South African artists decorate the open spaces inside the State Theatre. Classical musicals are often staged on Sunday afternoons; check the newspapers for details.

Pretoria Zoo ★★★

This is one of the largest of the world's zoological gardens, home to an extensive array of southern African and exotic animals, including the four great apes, the rare

MONUMENTS TO THE MOVERS

★★ The **Voortrekker Monument** commemorates the Great Trek – the mass movement of Boers from the British Cape Colony into the interior in the 1830s. It consists of a massive block ringed by 64 granite ox-wagons; one of the two great, decorated chambers inside bears a patriotic inscription commemorating the Boer victory over the Zulus at Blood River in 1838. An impressive monument, but it fits awkwardly into the new South Africa.
★★ The **Sammy Marks Museum**, on the east side of town, honours one of the previous century's greatest entrepreneurs; Swart-koppies Hall is a fine example of Victorian architecture, and opens onto a pleasant tea garden.

Opposite: *Pretoria's neo-classical Union Buildings have long been the head-quarters of the country's civil administration.* **Left:** *Jacaranda trees are characteristic of the city in spring, lining the roads with carpets of blossoms.*

PEACE AND QUIET

For a breath of fresh air and/or a look at wildlife, visit the:

** **National Botanical Garden**: more than 5,000 indigenous plant species and impressive herbarium.

** **Jan Smuts House**, Doornkloof, Irene: walk to the great man's grave on a hill with a panoramic view, enjoy tea in the garden afterwards.

** Gain wonderful view of the city from the **Moreleta Spruit trail** in the eastern suburb of Lynnwood Glen; leads through three bird-rich nature reserves.

* **Wonderboom Nature Reserve**, Voortrekker Road: 1,000-year-old, 23-m-tall (75 ft) wild fig 'wonder tree'.

TRAILING ARTS AND CRAFTS

About 20 km (12 miles) northwest of Johannesburg, the valley of the Crocodile River has attracted an unusual number of talented artists and craftspeople – painters, sculptors, potters, and workers in leather, stone, wood and textiles. Most of them keep open house on the first weekend of each month. Maps of and information on the **Crocodile River Arts and Crafts Ramble** are available from the Johannesburg Publicity Association.

South American maned wolf, a white tiger, and the only known giant eland in captivity in Africa. An aerial cableway takes visitors to the summit of a hill, from where they can view the wildlife in its natural habitat. The zoo also contains around 200 different kinds of bird, and there's a fascinating aquarium and reptile park. Carnivores are fed mid-afternoon, seals morning and afternoon.

Pick of the Museums

Kruger House at the corner of Church and Potgieter streets: the modest but charming residence of Paul Kruger (Transvaal president 1883-1900); it has been restored to its original character.

National Cultural History Museum in Boom Street: has a fine collection of Cape Dutch and 19th-century furniture, coins, medals and silverware; also archaeology and ethnology exhibits.

Transvaal Museum of Natural History: one-time headquarters of Robert Broom and other celebrated archaeologists; notable are displays of the man-apes, the bird hall, and the 'Life's Genesis' expo.

Melrose House in Jacob Maree Street: an elegant 19th-century home in attractive gardens; the peace treaty of Vereeniging, which ended the Anglo-Boer War in 1902, was signed here.

Pioneer Open-air Museum in Silverton: a Voortrekker farmstead typical of Pretoria's architecture in the 1850s.

DAY DRIVES FROM JOHANNESBURG AND PRETORIA

Hotel Aloe Ridge ★

On the West Rand, 45 kilometres (28 miles) from Johannesburg, the Aloe Ridge has a Zulu village adjacent, with accommodation in the form of authentic beehive huts. On neighbouring **Heia Safari Ranch**, a genuine 'braai' (barbecue) is accompanied by a 'Mzumba' traditional dance drama on Sundays; booking is essential.

Sterkfontein Caves ★

Not too far away, in the famed Sterkfontein caves, Dr Robert Broom's excavations yielded a million-year-

Left: *An Ndebele woman, flanked by the brightly patterned walling of her traditional home in the rural Transvaal region. The women are also renowned for their decorative, finely crafted beadwork.*

old fossilized cranium of ape-man *Australopithecus africanus*. The cathedral-like chambers and underground lake are eerie and fascinating; daily conducted tours.

Magaliesberg Hills ★

To the west of the Johannesburg–Pretoria axis, this ridge has a special woodland beauty all its own and, in the steeper places, even grandeur; it offers an inviting drive. To get there from Pretoria you must pass through the **Hartbeespoort Dam** recreational area (crowded at weekends). Consider staying overnight at the charming Mount Grace Country House or at Valley Lodge, and returning via the **Rustenburg Nature Reserve.**

Cheetah Research and Breeding Centre ★★

This centre 30 kilometres (19 miles) west of Pretoria is a rewarding outing for wildlife enthusiasts. Open on weekends, tours take place at 08:30 and 14:15. Nearby is the **Margaret Roberts Herbal Centre**, open to the public on Wednesdays only, picnicking permitted. Lectures on herbs are held on Tuesdays, workshops on Saturdays.

Carousel Entertainment World ★★

For bright lights and fun, the **Carousel** and nearby **Morula Sun** are only 25 minutes north of Pretoria, offering casinos, slots, restaurants and show bars. For more information, contact Sun International.

NDEBELE VILLAGES

Tourists interested in traditional African culture and lifestyles should visit the Ndebele village at **Loopspruit**, 55 km (28 miles) from Pretoria, which depicts the progression over the centuries of the Ndebele building style; open daily from 08:00 to 17:00. For further enquiries, contact KwaNdebele Tourism Board, tel: (01215) 47-2240.

Nearby is the **Loopspruit Wine Estate**, South Africa's northernmost wine producing area. Some of the wines have won awards. Conducted cellar tour, wine tasting and lunch offered, tel: (01212) 2-4303.

Exquisite examples of geometrically patterned Ndebele homes and intricate beadwork on women's costumes can also be viewed at the **Botshabelo Museum and Nature Reserve**, near Fort Merensky, 13 km (8 miles) north of Middelburg. Call (0132) 43-1319.

Sun City and Pilanesberg National Park
Sun City ★★★

Contrasting sharply with the surrounding arid countryside of **Bophuthatswana** is an enormous, extravagantly opulent complex of hotels, gaming rooms, theatres, restaurants, bars, discos and shops, all set in spacious and beautifully landscaped grounds.

This is the pleasure ground of Sun City, flagship of the prestigious Sun International hospitality group and mecca for both local and overseas holiday-makers. Cradled within the valley are four hotels, ranging from the family-oriented **Cabanas** through the plush, recently refurbished **Sun City** complex and the **Cascades** (whose foyer is cooled by a glistening veil of water spilling down one wall) to the magnificent **Palace of the Lost City**, which is inspired by a 'forgotten legend'.

THE PALACE OF THE LOST CITY

The **Palace**, an ornate affair of domes and minarets, forms the centrepiece of the multimillion-dollar Lost City development. It has 350 luxurious rooms and suites, two restaurants in fantasy settings of foliage and water and, in the grounds, a man-made jungle.

The **Valley of Waves**, an outdoor playground, incorporates waterfalls, lakes, river rides and an enormous surf pool with artificially generated waves.

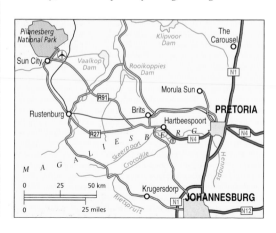

For golfers, there is a choice between the splendid Arizona desert-style golf course where crocodiles lie in wait at the 13th hole, and that at the Gary Player Country Club, which has hosted most of the world's greats and is the venue of the annual Million Dollar Golf Challenge.

Among Sun City's other outdoor amenities are riding stables and bowling greens, tennis and squash courts. Much revolves around the various and attractive stretches of water – the waterscape near the Cascades, with its interlinked pools, weirs, tropical walkways and waterfowl; and **Waterworld**, a giant man-made lake designed for both idlers and the water sportsman.

Well worth a visit is the nearby **Kwena Garden**, a 'prehistoric' reptile park and crocodile ranch. **Pilanesberg Safaris**, based at Sun City, organize game drives, guided walks and balloon safaris.

> ### STAYING IN THE PILANESBERG
>
> Accommodation ranges from the luxurious to cottages and caravan facilities. The top private lodges are:
> - **Kwa Maritane**: luxury hotel and timeshare complex; duplex cabanas and chalets with private patios.
> - **Bakubung**: similar to Kwa Maritane, but more affordable; thatched studio rooms and chalets; built around a hippo pool.
> - **Tshukudu**: luxury rest camp set on the crest of a ridge; self-contained chalets.

Pilanesberg National Park★★

Sun City is on the southern fringe of the Pilanesberg National Park, a great expanse of game-rich habitat that sprawls within four concentric mountain rings, relics of an aeons-old volcano; at the centre of the bowl is **Mankwe Lake**, which is home to hippo.

Some 10,000 head of game are found in the park, among them both the black and white rhino, giraffe and zebra, lion, cheetah, leopard, brown hyena, warthog and a wealth of antelope. More than 300 bird species have been identified, and a visit to the aviary at Manyane gate should not be missed. The Pilanesberg is traversed by an extensive network of game-viewing roads; conducted walks and drives are laid on, and hides have been established.

Opposite: *The opulent Palace hotel.* **Right:** *The Lost City's scallop-shaped Wave Pool.*

Johannesburg, Pretoria and Sun City at a Glance

BEST TIMES TO VISIT

Late spring (**September** and **October**) and autumn (**March** and **April**), when skies are usually clear, and temperatures warm.

GETTING THERE

The **international airport** is in Kempton Park, northeast of Johannesburg and southeast of Pretoria, and offers tourist information (Satour), 24-hour banking and currency exchanges, car hire, shopping, restaurant and bar facilities. Regular **bus service** connects airport with Rotunda in Leyd St, and six Sandton hotels.

GETTING AROUND

Johannesburg

Best to **hire a car**. City's layout fairly symmetrical – streets and urban freeway system run roughly east–west (M2) and north–south (M1); major routes well signposted and numbered. **Buses** adequate and inexpensive, but are essentially for commuters; regular services operate from around 20 designated areas on city's outskirts. **Taxi cabs** stick to ranks and are pricey, but most reliable are Rose's Taxis, tel: (011) 725-3333.

Pretoria

Pretoria's layout makes detailed map essential. **Airport bus** to Sammy Marks Square in city centre. Hotels offer **courtesy transport**. If you need a **taxi**, call Rixi, tel: (012) 325-8072.

Sun City

Many visitors fly in (scheduled air services from Jan Smuts airport); call Bop Air, tel: (011) 975-3901 or Sun International, tel: (011) 780-7800. Others come by **luxury coach** (daily service between Johannesburg and Sun City); contact Computicket, tel: (011) 331-9991, or your travel agent. **Helicopter transfers**: Court Helicopters, tel: (011) 827-8907. **By road**, Sun City is a two-hour drive from Johannesburg.

WHERE TO STAY

Johannesburg

Sandton Sun & Towers, Sandton, tel: (011) 780-5000, fax: 783-0421.
Balalaika Protea, Sandton, tel: (011) 884-1400, fax: 884-1463.
Rosebank Hotel, Rosebank, tel: (011) 788-1820, fax: 447-3276.
Sunnyside Park, Parktown, tel: (011) 643-7226, fax: 642-0019.
The Carlton and Carlton Court, central city, tel: (011) 331-8911, fax: 331-3555.

Pretoria

Karos Manhattan, tel: (012) 322-7635, fax: 320-0721.
Protea Hof, tel: (012) 322-9461, fax: 322-7570.
La Maison guest house, Hatfield, tel: (012) 43-4341, fax: 342-1531.
Centurion Lake Hotel, Verwoerdburg, 10 km south of Pretoria, tel: (012)

663-1825, fax: 663-2760.
Farm Inn, outside Pretoria, tel: (012) 807-0081, fax: 807-0088.

Pretoria North

Carousel Entertainment World, tel: (01464) 7-7777.
Morula Sun, tel: (011) 780-7800.

Magaliesberg

Mount Grace Country House, nestled in the hills, tel: (011) 880-1675.
Valley Lodge, has a new bird sanctuary, tel: (0142) 77-1301, fax: 77-1306.

Sun City and Pilanesberg

For accommodation in the Pilanesberg National Park, call **Golden Leopard Resorts** central reservations, tel: (011) 465-5423; for Sun City, tel: (011) 780-7800.

BUDGET ACCOMMODATION

Johannesburg

City Lodge Sandton (Katherine St), tel: (011) 444-5300, fax: 444-5315.
Jan Smuts City Lodge, tel: (011) 392-1750.
Jan Smuts Formule 1, tel: (011) 392-1453.
Sandton Holiday Inn, tel: (011) 783-5262, fax: 783-5289.

Pretoria

Garden Court Holiday Inn, city centre, tel: (012) 322-7500, fax: 322-9429.
Bed and Breakfast Pretoria, tel/fax: (012) 47-3597.

Johannesburg, Pretoria and Sun City at a Glance

Johannesburg

Ile de France: French provincial, rare oasis for gourmets, tel: (011) 706-2837.

Linger Longer: Georgian-style house, superlative cuisine, tel: (011) 884-0126.

Ma Cuisine: best haute cuisine out of France, tel: (011) 880-1946.

Sausalito: Californian, exotic ingredients and flavours, tel: (011) 783-3305.

The Baytree: French provincial, winner of many awards, tel: (011) 782-7219.

The Fisherman's Grotto: king of city's seafood restaurants, tel: (011) 834-6211.

Three Ships, Carlton Hotel: voted one of country's top three restaurants, tel: (011) 331-8911, ext 250.

Zoo Lake Restaurant: continental cuisine, pleasant views, tel: (011) 646-8807.

Ethnic restaurants

Gramadoelas at the Market: indigenous cuisine (Cape Malay to African traditional), tel: (011) 838-6960.

Leipoldt's: Cape Dutch fare, tel: (011) 339-2765.

Anton van Wouw, Doornfontein: splendid South African dishes, excellent game, tel: (011) 402-7916.

Pretoria

Chagall's at Toulouse, Fountains Valley: award-winner, as close to a Parisian restaurant as you can get, tel: (012) 341-7511.

Chatterley's, Church Street East: imaginative menu, tel: (012) 44-7920.

Chez Patrice, Riviera: consistently among Transvaal's top 10, tel: (012) 329-4028.

Hillside Tavern, Lynnwood: city's best steakhouse, tel: (012) 47-5119.

La Madeleine, Lynnwood Ridge: French-Belgian bistro, voted among top 10, tel: (012) 44-6076.

La Perla, Skinner Street: seafood a speciality, tel: (012) 322-2759.

Goldfields, State Theatre: exclusive, superb service and cuisine, tel: (012) 322-4147.

Ethnic restaurants

Diep in die Berg, Hans Strydom Avenue: game a speciality, tel: (012) 807-0111.

Gerard Moerdyk, Arcadia: very fine South African cuisine, tel: (012) 344-4856.

Bird's-eye view tours (city, mountains, game reserves), Court Helicopters, tel: (011) 827-8907; Gold Reef City Helicopters, tel: (011) 496-1400.

City and overland (Johannesburg), Action Tours, tel: (011) 783-4032; Jimmy's Face to Face Tours, tel: (011) 331-6109; Springbok Atlas, tel: (011) 493-0827; Welcome Tours and Safaris, tel: (011) 833-7030, ext 2398.

Heia Safari Ranch: tel: (011) 659-0605.

Hotel Aloe Ridge: tel: (011) 659-0605.

City and overland (Pretoria): Expeditionary Force (specializes in **historical tours** throughout southern Africa), tel: (012) 667-2833; Holidays for Africa, tel: (012) 83-1840; Jakaranda Tours, tel: (012) 807-1433; Sakabula Safaris & Tours, tel: (012) 98-1585.

Johannesburg Publicity Association, cnr Market and Kruis sts: 24-hour info service, tel: (011) 29-4961/4.

Carlton Hotel (for Soweto tours), tel: (011) 331-8911.

Pretoria Visitors' Bureau, Sammy Marks Square, tel: (012) 313-7980/7694.

Sun City and Pilanesberg

Pilanesberg Safaris: visit the safari desk at Sun City or call (014651) 2-1561.

Sun International central reservations, tel: (011) 780-7800, fax: 780-7449.

JOHANNESBURG	J	F	M	A	M	J	J	A	S	O	N	D
AVERAGE TEMP. °F	68	67	65	60	55	50	51	55	61	63	65	67
AVERAGE TEMP. °C	20	20	18	16	13	10	10	13	16	18	18	19
Hours of Sun Daily	8	8	8	8	9	9	9	10	9	9	8	8
RAINFALL in	5	4	3	2	1	0.5	0.5	0.5	1	3	4	4
RAINFALL mm	131	95	81	55	19	7	6	6	26	72	114	106
Days of Rainfall	15	11	11	9	4	2	1	2	3	10	14	14

3
Eastern Transvaal

Two hundred kilometres (125 miles) across the great highveld plateau east of the Johannesburg–Pretoria axis, the gently undulating grasslands give way to hills, and then to mountains that sweep up in a splendidly imposing ridge. This is the northern segment of the **Great Escarpment**. Scenically enchanting, the range rises near **Nelspruit**, the region's main town, and runs northeastwards for some 300 kilometres (185 miles).

The Escarpment's eastern faces are especially precipitous, falling to the heat-hazed, game-rich **Lowveld** plain that rolls away across the **Kruger National Park** and neighbouring Mozambique to the Indian Ocean.

TRANSVAAL ESCARPMENT

This is a land of marvellous diversity, a spectacular compound of forest-mantled massifs and high buttresses, sculpted peaks and deep ravines, crystal streams and delicate waterfalls, and of green valleys along which flow the Olifants and Crocodile rivers and their multiple tributaries. The uplands are not so dramatic as their counterparts to the south, the Natal Drakensberg (*see* p. 73); on the other hand, they're a lot more accessible to the ordinary traveller: the roads are in good condition, the hotels and hideaways plentiful and inviting.

Blyde River Canyon ★★★

Below the confluence of the Treur (sorrow) and Blyde (joy) rivers is one of Africa's great natural wonders: a massive and majestic red-sandstone gorge, whose cliff

Opposite: *The Lisbon Falls, a double waterfall near Graskop, is only one of the escarpment's myriad beautiful cascades. Nearby, Kowyn's Pass offers a spectacular throughway to the Lowveld plain below.*

DON'T MISS

*** Kruger National Park
*** MalaMala, Sabi Sabi
or Londolozi private
game reserves
*** Blyde River Canyon
*** Panorama and
Waterfall Routes
** Pilgrim's Rest historical
village.

ESCARPMENT TOWNS

Lydenburg is an attractive
and thriving town offering
all amenities (banks, shops
and hotels); the museum
and nature reserve nearby
are worth visiting. Higher up
the hills is **Sabie**, once a
gold town and now centre
of the forestry industry (the
museum has some fascinat-
ing exhibits). Nearby, on the
scenically stunning
Kowyn's Pass road, is the
pretty village of **Graskop**.
Southwest of Lydenburg is
Dullstroom, whose railway
station is the highest in
southern Africa. Dullstroom
has two enchanting little
hotels, much favoured by
fishermen (the area is
renowned for its trout
streams).

faces plunge almost sheer to the waters below. The 20-
kilometre-long (12 miles) gorge has been dammed to
create a lovely lake; at the top of the canyon there are
strategically sited viewing points, easily reached from the
main road, from which you gaze across the immensity of
the Lowveld plain and, closer, at the awesome massifs of
the **Mariepskop** and the **Three Rondavels**.

Much of the countryside around the gorge is occupied
by the **Blyderivierspoort Reserve**, known for its diverse
plant and bird life (which includes the imposing black
eagle, and the rare bald ibis which nests on the granite
cliffs), and a fine place for ramblers and horseback riders.
Within and just outside the reserve are two pleasant
resorts, a reptile park and **Bourke's Luck Potholes**, an
intriguing fantasia of water-fashioned rocks.

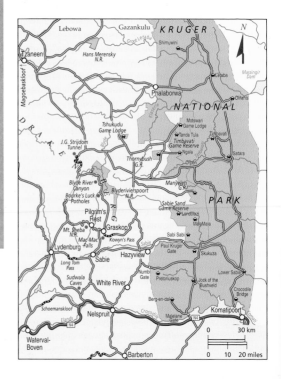

Opposite: *Part of the
Blyderivierspoort Nature
Reserve, a magnificent
upland sanctuary fringing
the Blyde River Canyon.*

WATERFALL ROUTE

The unofficial **Waterfall Route** takes in eight waterfalls in the Sabie-Graskop vicinity. The most attractive waterfalls are:
- **Bridal Veil** (aptly named)
- **Mac-Mac** with its twin cataracts; drops into dense ravine, then runs into the exquisite Mac-Mac Pools
- **Lone Creek**, 68 m (222 ft); the mist-forest is a joy
- **Horseshoe**, a national monument
- **Berlin** plunges 48 m (158 ft) into a deep pool
- **Lisbon**, a double waterfall in a setting of special beauty.

The last two have observation points and picnic sites.

Perhaps the most breathtaking view site in the entire Escarpment is **God's Window**, a gap in the high mountain rampart near the southern extremity of the reserve.

Pilgrim's Rest ★★★

When gold was discovered on the Escarpment in 1873, the itinerant diggers flocked in, setting up camps at Spitzkop and Mac-Mac (Scotsmen featured prominently in the rush) and, later, after an even richer strike, at Pilgrim's Rest, so named because here, after so many false trails and faded dreams, the gold-hunting fraternity finally found a permanent home.

The camp flourished: tents and shacks were replaced by iron-roofed cottages, traders and canteen owners set up shop, a church and a newspaper made their appearance, the **Royal Hotel** opened its hospitable doors, and for some years the little frontier settlement enjoyed itself to the full, sometimes in outrageous style. Eventually, though, the alluvial gold ran out and syndicates and companies were formed to dig deeper. The last of the mines closed in the 1970s, although long before then (in the 1940s) the owners had spread their investments, diversifying into timber. Some of the world's largest man-made forests (pine and wattle) now mantle the slopes of the Escarpment.

Pilgrim's Rest isn't your standard ghost town. It still supports a few hundred permanent residents, and its charming early character (1880-1915) has been carefully preserved to allow the place to function as a 'living museum'. The Royal still plays host to visitors; its pub – the fittings of which once graced a chapel in far-off Lourenço Marques (now Maputo) until 1893, when they were hauled over the mountain to serve an entire-

ly different type of congregation – is well patronized; and the rooms you sleep in are very much as they were a century ago. Also available to guests are some of the original miners' cottages, and there are guided tours of the village, of the **Diggers' Museum** (which gives gold-panning demonstrations) and of **Alanglade**, the opulently furnished home of an early mine manager.

SCENIC DAY DRIVES

Panorama Route ★★★

Wherever you go on the Escarpment, you'll find scenic riches and splendid view sites. The circular Panorama Route is especially inviting. Beginning and ending in Sabie, it takes in the Mac-Mac and Lisbon falls, God's Window, the Berlin Falls, a fern-festooned picnic site in the nature reserve, Bourke's Luck Potholes, Blyde River Canyon, the valley of Pilgrim's Creek and Pilgrim's Rest.

Long Tom Pass ★★

Another spectacular escarpment drive winds through **Robber's Pass** and the **Long Tom Pass**. The latter, named after the giant Boer siege-gun that plagued the British during the 1899-1902 war, has especially steep and tortuous gradients. It is notable for its grand vistas, for The

Knuckles (four peaks in a row) and for The Staircase, which defeated many a wagon in the early days.

A digression south of the Robber's Pass road will lead you down a steep, rugged track to one of the Eastern Transvaal's finest private nature reserves, **Mount Sheba**. The indigenous forest here is part of an extraordinarily stable floral community that, together with the area's animals and birds, forms a coherent ecosystem; more than 1,000 different plants have been identified. Paths have been laid out, some leading to old mine workings. Mountain biking and trout fishing are available.

Magoebaskloof ★★

To the northwest, across the Olifants River and on for a further 150 kilometres (90 miles), is the attractively tropical farming town of **Tzaneen**, and just beyond, the densely wooded, misty, magical heights of the **Magoebaskloof**. The pass is accessible via a good but very steep road, affording grand views over the surrounding uplands, and the plantations and patches of indigenous forest they sustain. The loveliest of these is perhaps the **Woodbush**, which visiting novelist John Buchan described as 'the extreme of richness and beauty'. It is home to giant yellowwoods, ironwoods, stinkwoods and other splendid species. A couple of hotels in the area are excellent; Tzaneen itself and the nearby **Modjadji cycad forest** are also worth exploring.

> **GOING UNDERGROUND**
>
> The **Echo complex**, north of Lydenburg, is an intriguing sequence of caverns that echo with disproportionate loudness when you tap their stalagmites and stalactites. The caves were once home to stone-age peoples; you can see relics of their occupation – rock paintings and excavated sites – at the nearby **Museum of Man**.
> More impressive is the **Sudwala system** to the south, a network of caverns thought to burrow through the dolomite for 30 km (19 miles) in a series of linked chambers. The nearby **dinosaur park** displays life-sized replicas of the creatures that roamed this part of the earth 250 million years ago.

Left: *Souvenir sellers lend a splash of bright colour to the main tourist routes.*
Opposite: *The main street of Pilgrim's Rest, whose Victorian dwellings have been beautifully preserved.*

Above: *The Eastern Transvaal's tortuous Long Tom Pass was originally built with pick and shovel.*

BEST BUYS

The richly productive farming areas around Nelspruit and White River have given rise to a proliferation of colourful wayside stalls selling fresh, seasonal produce as well as interesting curios. Look out for:

• **Luscious tropical fruits** (mangoes, litchis, pineapples, pawpaws, avocados)
• **Pecan nuts**
• **Macadamia nuts**
• **Hand-woven rugs**
• **Leather goods**
• **Hand carvings**

TRANSVAAL LOWVELD

The low-lying plain below the Escarpment is occupied in large part by the Kruger National Park and bordering private reserves; however an important agricultural industry flourishes around the towns of Nelspruit and White River, in the fertile Crocodile River Valley, where farmlands yield an abundance of subtropical fruits, vegetables and tobacco.

Towns of the Lowveld

Largest of the region's centres, **Nelspruit** is a prosperous-looking place of wide streets, clean-lined buildings and tree-garlanded suburbs. It's the last major stop on the main west–east highway from Johannesburg and Pretoria, and the jumping-off point for visitors arriving by both road and air.

Among the town's attractions are good hotels and restaurants, sophisticated shops and speciality outlets. Make an effort to visit the **Lowveld Botanical Gardens** on the banks of the Crocodile River, which is known for its fascinating array of local, mainly subtropical, plants.

Of particular interest – to the layman as well as the botanist – is the herbarium.

To the north of Nelspruit is **White River**, a little country town attractively placed among some of South Africa's richest farming lands: more than 3,000 smallholders grow flowers, pecan and macadamia nuts, and tropical fruits, among other things.

On the other side of Nelspruit, in the steamy De Kaap Valley, lies **Barberton**, yet another Transvaal town founded on gold. The first deposits were discovered in 1883 and, while the reef still yielded its treasure, it was a large and lively settlement – a typical Wild West-type boom town of shanties, music halls, hotels, two stock exchanges and scores of drinking dens. The 'Barberton Bubble' burst soon enough, and the town is much quieter now, but a few hints of the romantic past linger, best seen perhaps in the elegant **Belhaven House Museum**.

KRUGER NATIONAL PARK

Teeming with game, the Kruger National Park and the extensive private reserves that fringe the park's western boundary represent the 'real' Africa. South Africa's premier game sanctuary covers nearly 20,000 square kilo-

THE KRUGER'S BIG FIVE IN BIRDS

For the bird-watcher, about 500 species have been recorded in the park, including some superb raptors (Wahlberg's eagle, the bateleur and five species of vulture among them). In the rest camps many bird species are confiding and approachable. On your outings, watch out for the following Big Five, easily identifiable and the chances of spotting them are good:
- **Saddlebilled stork**
- **Lappetfaced vulture**
- **Martial eagle**
- **Kori bustard**
- **Ground hornbill**

Below: *Game-viewing in Kruger National Park; the region is crisscrossed by an extensive network of well-maintained roads.*

KMV976T

FACTS ABOUT THE KRUGER

The park is named after **Paul Kruger**, president of the first South African Republic, who established the Sabie Game Reserve in 1898. A second reserve (Shingwedzi) was proclaimed in 1903, and the two were combined and renamed Kruger National Park. **James Stevenson-Hamilton** was appointed as the first curator. A dedicated conservationist (his black staff called him 'Skukuza' – he who sweeps clean – for his tireless campaign against poaching), the park was elevated to the foremost ranks of the world's wilderness areas during his period in office.

A commemorative trail pays tribute to **Sir Percy FitzPatrick**, a one-time trader who plied the Eastern Transvaal route during the gold rush. His adventures with his dog are immortalized in his famous book *Jock of the Bushveld*.

metres (7,720 square miles) of the Lowveld between the Crocodile River in the south and the Limpopo (the border with Zimbabwe) in the north.

The busy park contains around 5,000 visitors at any given time; comfort and easy access to the array of wildlife are the keynotes, and there's very little of the classic African safari about your stay here. The rest camps are pleasant, tree-shaded and well-founded oases in a bushveld setting, linked by an extensive network of good roads; within leisurely driving distance of each camp are water holes, view sites, picnic spots and a wealth of wildlife and scenic interest.

Fortunately, the Kruger's sheer size ensures that it remains unspoilt. Everything introduced by man – the camps, the designated stopping areas, the routes and the 'visual bands' that run along either side of them – takes up less than three per cent of the area; the other 97 per cent belongs to nature.

The Wildlife

The Kruger National Park boasts the greatest species diversity in Africa, due to the fact that the area encompasses many different habitats. Among the nearly 140 resident mammal species are the 'big five': lion (of which there are about 1,500); elephant (around 8,000); leopard (around 1,000 although difficult to spot); buffalo (an

impressive 25,000, often seen in herds of up to 200); and rhino, of both the white and black varieties. Both the last-mentioned are classed as endangered; the black rhino is especially vulnerable to poachers. Other large game populations include more than 30,000 zebra, 14,000 wildebeest and 5,000 giraffe; hippo and crocodile can be seen in numbers in and around the rivers; antelope in their thousands roam the grasslands; and the park remains one of the few places in South Africa where wild dog can be seen in its natural environment.

All these forms of life, together with the reptiles and amphibians, the trees (400 different types, including baobabs, fever trees, marulas and mopanes; tree lists are available), shrubs and grasses and the uncountable insects and micro-organisms, combine to create a wonderfully coherent habitat, a system of gene pools in perfect (though fragile) balance, and in which the cycle of life is sustained by collective dependence.

The Rest Camps

There are over 20 **camps** scattered throughout Kruger Park, all pleasantly restful, fenced against the animals and neatly laid out, most of them graced by lovely indigenous trees, flowering plants and expanses of lawn. Five are classed as **bushveld camps** which comprise fully equipped, serviced huts, slightly larger than the normal

CREEPY-CRAWLIES

About a quarter of South Africa's 100 or so snake species can inflict a dangerous bite, among them the adder, mamba, cobra and boomslang. Most rest camps and lodges keep a store of anti-snake bite serum.

The majority of South Africa's 5,000 spider species are entirely harmless; most dangerous is the button spider, though even its bite is rarely fatal. Scorpion bites can be more painful, but are also rarely dangerous to man. Common in the bushveld is a small, red tick that can, if infected, transmit the typhus-type tick-bite fever. The condition is treatable.

Right: *The pleasantly shady Shingwedzi rest camp, in the north-central region, is famed for its birdlife.* **Opposite:** *With its elegant, long neck, the giraffe is able to nibble at the tender shoots that are out of reach for most other herbivores.*

LOWVELD HEALTH HAZARDS

Malaria is prevalent in the region all year round, but especially in summer (September to April). Take a course of prophylactic tablets before your departure: they're available without prescription at pharmacies throughout the country. In recent years, drug-resistant strains of malaria have become cause for concern; the best advice is to try and avoid being bitten by mosquitos.

There is also **bilharzia** (known too as *schistosomiasis*), a debilitating waterborne disease caused by a parasitical worm that inhabits low-lying rivers and dams. Avoid swimming or paddling in slow-running and still water unless there are clear assurances that they're bilharzia free.

Above: *Juvenile lions survey their terrain from a rocky vantage point; these powerful cats are superb hunters, but drought and disease take a heavy toll, especially among the young.* **Opposite:** *Ancient baobab trees feature prominently among the Kruger Park's acacia and mopane vegetation.*

accommodation; five more comprise **private** clusters of huts and chalets available on a block-booking basis.

Accommodation is comfortable and spacious: a typical family cottage has two bedrooms including bedding, a bathroom, a toilet, a small kitchen (with refrigerator, gas stove, utensils, cutlery and crockery provided), a gauzed-in verandah, air conditioning and a barbecue site outside. Lower down the scale are huts without kitchens but communal facilities are available; top of the range are the guest cottages, privately owned but available for hire and, some of them, exceedingly well appointed.

Camp routine is relaxed and undemanding, the emphasis on low-cost outdoor living. Visitors usually cook their own meals, though all the larger venues have public restaurants, informal eating places that serve adequate food in a friendly atmosphere. Many are strategically sited to overlook a river or a water hole.

Select Camps

Skukuza, the park's headquarters: more of a busy little village than a conventional bush camp. It has all the tourist amenities, including two restaurants, airline and car-hire offices, a supermarket, petrol and service station, a doctor's surgery, an information centre, an exhibition hall, a golf course, and a nursery that sells palms, cycads, baobabs and other indigenous plants.

Lower Sabie: located in an area especially rich in wildlife (buffalo, lion and a myriad antelope); has a lovely setting of lawns and shade trees.

Berg-en-Dal: naturally landscaped modern camp (maximum use of local materials has been made); accommodation is well spaced out for privacy; beautiful trees.

Satara: large, with very attractive grounds that are home to a great many birds; the area teems with wildlife.

Olifants: sited on a cliff edge, has spectacular views of the game-rich river valley below, and beyond to the hills.

Letaba: very handsome, sited above a sweeping bend in the Letaba River; sundowners on the terrace fill a magical hour. Don't miss out on a visit to the Gold Fields Centre Elephant Museum, which has interesting exhibits.

Mopani: newish luxury camp, cleverly designed to blend in with the natural surrounds; offers good views; bungalows are built from stone and thatch.

Shingwedzi: one of the best camps for bird-watchers (keep your eyes peeled for the pearlspotted owl and the

ON SAFARI: WHAT TO PACK

In the bushveld, nobody dresses up, and most of the larger rest camps and private lodges have laundry facilities, which means you could probably get away with just two changes of clothes. Avoid bright colours and white; neutral hues are best for game-viewing and bird-watching. Nights can be chilly, even bitterly cold in winter: pack a warm sweater, tracksuit or anorak. Among other items in your luggage will be a swimming costume, a sun hat, stout walking shoes, personal toiletries that include lip salve and sun-protection cream, good sunglasses, insect repellent, a torch (fitted with new batteries), binoculars, and bird, mammal and tree field-guides.

RAIL SAFARI TO BIG-GAME COUNTRY

Over weekends during winter, the luxury **Blue Train** runs between Pretoria and Nelspruit, crossing the scenic route in about six hours. From there, you are whisked off to an exciting game lodge, or you can embark on a tour through the lovely Escarpment area. For information, call (011) 773-7621.

The equally de luxe **Rovos Rail** steam-train excursion, which also begins in Pretoria, undertakes a four-day (return) trip through the Eastern Transvaal's spectacular mountains and pine plantations, before descending to the Lowveld, where guests are transported to Kruger Park. For information, tel: (012) 323-6052.

mourning dove); known for its magnificent elephants.
Punda Maria: northernmost camp; has more than the usual wilderness feel about it; charming and sociable.

The above camps each have a restaurant and shops.

PRIVATE GAME RESERVES

The Kruger National Park takes up a large portion of the Lowveld, but by no means all of it. Sprawled along its west–central boundary are the **Timbavati**, **Manyeleti** and **Sabie Sand** reserves, three of the world's largest private game sanctuaries. Fences between the national park and its neighbours have been removed, and the animals are free to roam at will over the combined wilderness area.

The reserves embrace a score or so luxury game lodges, each with its individual character and special appeal. Most are supremely comfortable and beautifully run, and most of the resident rangers are young, charming, helpful and immensely knowledgeable about the ways of the wild.

Lodge meals are both ample and good. The traditional evening 'braai' (barbecue) is memorable; this is held under the stars, in the firelit, reed-enclosed *boma*, with the night-time sounds of Africa all around you; the atmos-

phere is informal and cheerful, the company entertaining, and the evenings often turn into a roaring party.

Much of your day – all but the hottest hours – is spent in a Land-Rover in the company of a ranger–tracker team. The trips provide endless fascination: the team's bushcraft skills are remarkable, the search (for, say, the spoor of lion) exacting, the first sight of the quarry exhilarating. There are also night excursions, guided walks through the bush and, for the more patient, strategically placed hides overlooking a water hole.

LUXURY LODGES

- **Inyati**, thatched camp on the banks of the Sand River
- **Londolozi**, two well-appointed camps, chalets each with private verandah
- **MalaMala**, five camps, from top of the range to the real wilderness experience
- **Motswari** and **M'Bali**, charming rondavels and 'habi-tents' (luxury rooms on a platform)
- **Ngala**, upmarket, elegant chalets, luxury private suite
- **Sabi Sabi**, two camps, one on the river bank, one in the bushveld.
- **Ulusaba**, two ultraluxurious lodges, one built into the edge of the mountain.

Opposite: *The Kruger Park's secluded Bateleur bush camp.* **Above:** *The nocturnal leopard, perfectly at home in the branches of a tree.* **Left:** *Typical Kruger landscape.*

Eastern Transvaal at a Glance

Summer in the **Lowveld** very hot and humid; winter days pleasant and sunny (temperatures remain in the 20s), making this the perfect time to visit (**June/July**). Though the countryside is drier, the aloes are resplendent.

The **Transvaal Escarpment**'s higher altitude ensures a kind climate year-round, though summer brings swathes of mists that affect the views. Best times between **October** and **January**, before the onset of the rains.

Kruger Park

Winter months (**June** to **August**) are best for game-viewing – trees have lost their leaves, the grass is short, the earth dry, so wildlife tends to congregate around the water holes. In contrast, summer brings life-giving rains, rivers flow, pools fill and bushveld takes on rich luxuriance, but it is also harder to locate and observe wildlife. Towards the end of **November** and **early December**, you will probably see newborns. Malaria is prevalent at this time of the year, so ensure you take the necessary precautions.

Nelspruit's **airport** 8 km (5 miles) from centre, with regular flights to and from Johannesburg and Durban. Small **air charters** also operate between airport and various game reserves.

Kruger Park

By air: Most overseas visitors fly in, either independently or on a package tour. Comair flies direct to Skukuza from Johannesburg; regular scheduled flights from Durban and Johannesburg to Nelspruit and Phalaborwa (Metavia, Air Link). From here, **car hire** services available; minibuses are recommended for game-viewing.

By road: For those who prefer to drive, access routes are excellent; Kruger Park is a comfortable four-hour journey from Johannesburg or Pretoria.

The park has eight entrance gates; petrol outlets at six of them and at larger rest camps. In the interests of safety (yours and that of the animals) travel inside the park is restricted to daylight hours; gates and camps have set opening and closing hours which vary slightly with the season; two camps operate breakdown services. Nelspruit, as the major stop-off point between the Johannesburg–Pretoria and Lowveld–Eastern Escarpment areas, is linked to the major cities by a sophisticated highway system. Enormously popular tourist venue, especially during Transvaal school holidays (early **December** to **mid-January**, first three weeks of **April** and most of **July**);

advisable to book accommodation well in advance. Reservations can be made through travel agent, or contact National Parks Board, PO Box 787, Pretoria 0001, tel: (012) 343-1991. There is also a regional office in Cape Town, tel: (021) 419-5365.

Pamphlets and brochures describing facilities available; also excellent guidebooks.

Transvaal Escarpment
Böhm's Zeederberg Guest House, between Sabie and Hazyview: German-style *gasthaus* in pine forests, well placed for both Escarpment and Lowveld, tel: (01317) 6-8101, fax 6-8193.
Mount Sheba, west of Pilgrim's Rest: luxury hotel and time-share complex, set in exquisite forest reserve, tel/fax: (01315) 8-1241.
Blydepoort, perched at rim of Blyde River Canyon: sweeping views, self-contained chalets and luxury cottages, call Aventura Resorts, tel: (012) 346-2277.

Northern Transvaal
Glenshiel Country Lodge, Magoebaskloof: gracious, set in rolling hills and meadows, tel: (011) 788-1258, fax: 788-0789.
Troutwaters Inn, Magoebaskloof: resort overlooking trout-filled dam, tel: (015272), ask for 80, fax: ask for 53, then ask to be connected.

Eastern Transvaal at a Glance

Trout Fishing Lodges

Bergwaters, Waterval Onder: quiet retreat in Elands River valley, old-fashioned hospitality, country cooking, tel: (013262), ask for 103.

Critchley Hackle Lodge, Dullstroom: peaceful, stone-built complex at lake's edge, personalized service, tel: (01325) 4-0145, fax: 4-0262.

Sabie Townhouse, Sabie: set in lush gardens with stunning views across Sabie gorge, falls nearby, tel: (01315) 4-2292, fax: 5-0729.

Walkerson Collection, Dullstroom: thatch-and-stone manor, views across lake and forest, tel: (01325) 4026, fax: 4-0260.

Transvaal Lowveld

Cybele Forest Lodge, White River: set in woodland, one of the very best, beautiful rooms, superb cuisine, tel: (01311) 5-0511, fax: 3-2839.

Farmhouse Country Lodge, between White River and Hazyview: thatched luxury suites with magnificent views, lavish farm-fresh meals, tel: (01317) 6-8780, fax: 6-8783.

Highgrove House, between White River and Hazyview: colonial-style farmhouse in garden surrounds, breakfast under a gazebo, tel: (01311) 5-0242, fax: 5-0244.

Casa do Sol, between Hazyview and Sabie: imaginative Mediterranean-style complex of cobbled walkways, archways and fountains, tel/fax: (01317) 6-8111.

Jatinga Country Lodge, White River: 1920s homestead with river frontage, candlelight dining, tel: (01311) 3-1932, fax: 3-2364.

Old Joe's Kaia, Schoemanskloof Valley: rustic log cabins in subtropical gardens, lamplit dinners, picnicking at river's edge, tel/fax: (01311) 6-3045.

Kruger National Park

For all accommodation, call **National Parks Board,** tel: (012) 343-1991; Cape Town, tel: (021) 419-5365.

Private Game Reserves

Inyati, tel: (011) 493-0755, fax: 493-0837.

Londolozi, tel: (011) 803-8421, fax: 803-1810.

MalaMala, tel: (011) 789-2677, fax: 886-4382.

Motswari/M'Bali, tel: (011) 463-1990, fax: 463-1992.

Ngala, tel: (011) 803-8421, fax: 803-1810.

Sabi Sabi, tel: (011) 483-3939, fax: 483-3799.

Ulusaba, tel: (011) 465-4240, fax: 465-6649.

WHERE TO EAT

Guests at any of the lodges or private game reserves are fully catered for, the cuisine usually excellent. Picnic lunches are often provided if prior notice is given. Generally, lodges will accept dinner guests not staying at the lodge itself, but reservations are essential. Larger resorts normally have restaurant facilities.

TOURS AND EXCURSIONS

There are no organized bus tours from Nelspruit.

Coach tours throughout the Eastern Transvaal start from Johannesburg, and are arranged by Springbok Atlas, tel: (011) 493-3780, and Translux, tel: (011) 774-3333; or call Lowveld Promotions, tel: (01311) 2-6108.

River rafting on Sabie River, tel: Luthusaba Ventures, Hazyview, tel: (01317) 67299.

USEFUL CONTACTS

Lydenburg Tourist Information, Town Clerk's Office, Lydenburg, tel: (01323) 2121.

Nelspruit Publicity Office/Satour Information, Shop 5, Promenade Centre, Louis Trichardt St, tel: (01311) 55-1988.

Sondela Tourist Information, Main St at Old Trading Post, Sabie, tel: (01315) 4-3492.

NELSPRUIT	J	F	M	A	M	J	J	A	S	O	N	D
AVERAGE TEMP. °F	75	74	73	69	63	59	59	63	66	70	72	73
AVERAGE TEMP. °C	24	24	29	21	18	15	15	7	20	21	22	23
Hours of Sun Daily	7	7	7	7	8	8	9	9	8	7	6	6
RAINFALL in	5	5	4	2	1	0.5	0.5	0.5	11	2.5	4.5	5
RAINFALL mm	130	119	98	47	19	10	10	10	29	65	114	13
Days of Rainfall	13	12	10	7	4	2	3	3	5	9	13	13

4
Natal

Known as the 'garden province' of South Africa, Natal is a well-watered land of rolling green hills and a magnificent Indian Ocean coastline that stretches some 600 kilometres (370 miles) from Mozambique in the north to Transkei in the south. Much of the region's northern half is occupied by the historic territory of **Zululand**; inland, the countryside rises to the foothills and then to the massive heights of the Great Escarpment, here known as the **Natal Drakensberg** (dragon mountain).

Durban is the province's largest city; **Pietermaritzburg**, in the misty uplands 90 kilometres (56 miles) to the west, the provincial capital.

Natal's rural economy is based on the vast sugarcane plantations along its seaboard; other major commodities include tropical and subtropical fruits (pineapples, bananas), dairy products, timber and maize. Coal is mined in great quantities in the Newcastle area.

Seventy-five per cent of Natalians are **Zulus**, 15 per cent are **Indians**, and **white** people account for about 10 per cent of the population.

DURBAN

South Africa's third largest metropolis, after Johannesburg and Cape Town, and foremost seaport (the harbour is Africa's biggest and busiest and is ranked ninth in the world), Durban began life as the remote trading and white-hunter outpost of Port Natal. Today the city sprawls along the coast to the south, across the Umgeni

CLIMATE

Natal's **subtropical** climate is kind to holiday-makers throughout the seasons. Rainfall is generous, especially during summer. At this time, the air along the coastal belt is **hot** and **humid** – oppressively so in the weeks around Christmas. Inland, though, the heat usually stays within comfortable limits. Durban enjoys an average daily maximum temperature in January (high summer) of just over 27 °C (81 °F) and a July (winter) daily maximum of 22 °C (72 °F).

Opposite: *Durban's elegant seafront, mecca for tens of thousands of summertime sun and fun lovers.*

DON'T MISS

*** Natal game reserves
(Umfolozi, Hluhluwe, Mkuzi
and Ndumo)
*** Phinda Reserve
An ecotourist haven
*** The Drakensberg
A magnificent mountain
range
** Shakaland   A splendid
re-creation of Zulu lifestyles.

BEST BEACHES

Durban is known for its
broad, sweeping beaches,
especially those along the
Golden Mile.
  These can be uncomfort-
ably crowded, especially in
the weeks before and over
the Christmas period, as
swimmers, surfers and sun
worshippers flock to the
surf. The waters are warm,
the rollers often challenging; the shore from
Addington to **Blue
Lagoon** (and many of those
farther up and down the
coast) is protected by shark
nets and patrolled by lifeguards and beach
constables.
  The **Bay of Plenty** on the
Golden Mile is the venue for
the annual international
Gunston 500 surfing
competition.

River in the north, and up the Berea, a ridge of hills that overlooks the city centre, the beachfront and the bay.

As one of the country's popular holiday destinations, it is well known for its surf and its beaches. Durban's hotels and restaurants, nightspots, discos, shopping malls, parks and playgrounds are geared for the holidaymaker in search of sun-filled leisure and frivolous fun. The city offers the tourist, among other attractions: viewing galleries of the harbour and city at **Ocean Terminal**; pleasure cruises, departing from the **Dick King** jetty; features of interest on the **Victoria Embankment,** including the **Da Gama** clock and the **Dick King** statue (in commemoration of the Briton who in 1842 undertook an epic ride to seek help after British troops were surrounded by soldiers of the new Boer Republic of Natalia); and the nearby **Port Natal Maritime Museum**.

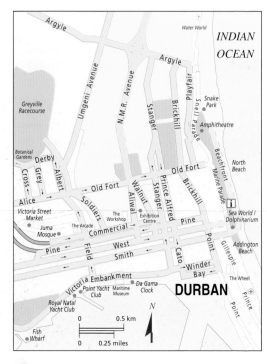

Opposite: *Crystal-clear paddling pools on Durban's Golden Mile, a kaleidoscope of gaiety and colour.*

The Golden Mile ★★★

Durban's beachfront, known as the **Golden Mile**, stretches six kilometres (four miles) along the sandy Indian Ocean shoreline and it offers much to the hedonist: paddling pools, pavilions, piers, playgrounds, amusement parks, round-the-clock eating places and nightclubs, neon-lit entertainment centres, emporiums and colourful markets, wide beaches and emerald lawns, and graceful walkways and broad thoroughfares that lead past some of Africa's most elegant hotels.

Among the strip's special features are the **rickshas**, lightly built carts pulled by Zulu 'drivers', both elaborately decked out in beads, furs and streamers. In the early days they were the standard means of about-town transport but today only a few remain, serving mainly as a tourist attraction.

Worth visiting is the **Fitzsimon's Snake Park** on Snell Parade, North Beach: it contains a fine collection of exotic and indigenous species plus crocodiles, leguaans (iguanas) and terrapins. Open daily, demonstrations are held four times a day in the tourist season; feeding time for the snakes and crocodiles occurs over the weekend.

Right: Dolphins go through their paces at Sea World; the impressive oceanarium also features sharks.

OCEANARIUM

At the bottom of West Street is **Sea World**, one of South Africa's leading marine-research centres, and home to the Oceanographic Research Institute. The showcase **aquarium** and **dolphinarium** house a wondrous array of marine fish, stingrays, turtles and sharks, and a fantasia of corals, anemones and seashells. Twice a day divers enter the giant tank to hand-feed the residents.

PEACE AND QUIET

- **Bluff Nature Reserve** in Jacobs: one of Durban's best bird-watching spots.
- **Botanical Gardens** in Lower Berea: indigenous flora, an orchid house and herbarium, and a garden for the blind.
- **Beachwood Mangroves Nature Reserve**, north of Durban: one of the area's last mangrove swamps.
- **Krantzkloof Nature Reserve**: a place of deep gorges, streams, waterfalls and forest; features rare plant and bird species.
- **Umgeni River Bird Park**: rated third among the world's bird parks, with 400 exotic and local species in huge, walk-through aviaries.

One of Durban's newest shopping complexes is **The Wheel**, a lively collection of speciality shops, restaurants, bars and cinemas in Gillespie Street and Point Road (it takes its name from the huge and glitzy ferris wheel that decorates the façade). Interior decor is thematic: part of the second floor resembles a casbah, the movie level is Caribbean, the ground floor nautical (there are flags, rigging and lifeboats, the flooring is planked deck, the walls are bulkheads, and ships' railings separate the shops).

For those who need a break from the noise and bustle, take a stroll to the **Amphitheatre** on Marine Parade (opposite the lavish Elangeni Hotel) – a sunken area of quiet lawns, flowers and fountains, footbridges and gazebos. A colourful flea market is held here every Sunday; traditional dances are performed and exotic dishes served on international theme days.

Access to the Golden Mile can be difficult during the holiday season. The area is packed with people and cars; only the lucky find parking spaces. The best ways to get there from the city centre are by taxi, by conventional bus, by the Mynah minibus shuttle service, or by the Tuk-Tuk three-wheelers that travel through the city to points along the beachfront. Or make your way there on foot: much of the strip is within comfortable walking distance of the central area – though not in the sweltering heat of a midsummer's day (between December and March).

Shopping

Durban's main shopping area is the Central Business District (CBD). Elsewhere, notable outlets include the imaginative and fun **Workshop**, a large Victorian structure – once the railway workshops – that houses 120 speciality shops (many of them replicas of early colonial houses), barrow stalls and eating places; **The Wheel** on the Golden Mile (*see* opposite); **The Arcade**, opposite Pine Parkade, consisting of upmarket speciality shops; and the new **Pavilion** shopping mall (has an Eastern flavour) in Westville, 15 minutes out of the city. There are various flea markets, among them, one in the vicinity of The Workshop, one in the Amphitheatre (*see* opposite) and one on the **South Plaza** of the **Exhibition Centre**.

A SMALL CORNER OF INDIA

A few blocks to the west of the city centre is a colourful and exotic world of mosques and temples, where bright saris mingle with the more prosaic styles of the West. The focal point is the **Victoria Street Indian Market**, a large and busy place of bargain and barter housed in a huge domed building. Examples of Indian cultural heritage accessible to the ordinary visitor include:

- **Juma Mosque** (the southern hemisphere's largest) in Grey Street
- **Hare Krishna Temple of Understanding** (Hindu)
- **Durban Hindu Temple**
- **Shree Shiva Subrahmanya Alayam**.

The best way to see something of this fascinating world is to join the Oriental Walkabout tour (*see* p. 81).

Right: *Durban city is noted for its unusually wide thoroughfares, of which West Street ranks among the most attractive; it was named after Martin West, first lieutenant-governor of Natal.*

Above: *One of Durban's few remaining rickshas and its decorated Zulu 'driver'.*

Museums, Galleries, Theatres and Exhibitions

Local History Museum in Aliwal Street: offers an intriguing insight into Natal's lively past.

Natural Science Museum and **Durban Art Gallery** in the City Hall: the art gallery features a permanent collection of South African contemporary, European and Oriental works.

African Art Centre nearby, off Gardiner Street: nonprofit enterprise, functions as part shop and part gallery of Zulu arts and crafts and is housed in a building that has been described as 'one of the real treasures of Durban'.

Killie Campbell Museum, corner of Essenwood and Marriott roads: comprises an exhibition of Nataliana, set in lovely grounds.

Natal Playhouse: an architecturally inspiring theatre complex which, despite a major fire, has retained its Tudor and Moorish-style façades. It houses five theatres, catering to all tastes of entertainment.

North Coast

The upmarket resort area of **Umhlanga Rocks** to the north of Durban boasts fine beaches, luxury hotels, holiday homes and apartments, excellent shops, and 30-plus restaurants. It is known for its safe bathing (to the north of the lighthouse), excellent surfing and its plethora of visitor amenities. The **La Lucia** residential suburb is one of the region's most fashionable. The **Dolphin Coast**, quieter than the south, stretches for 90 kilometres (55 miles) just north of Umhlanga up to the **Tugela River** mouth. You can travel on either the N2, or the more interesting Old North Road (R102) which runs a few kilometres inland. It follows the trade routes once used by the Zulu *impis*, and now serves the vast plantations and 'sugar towns' of the region, of which **Tongaat** is the 'capital'.

South Coast

Amanzimtoti is a substantial resort town (it has an extensive business district) that offers a wide range of holiday accommodation, restaurants, bars, entertainment, marvellous stretches of sand (two main beaches are manned by professional lifeguards all year round), a lagoon and tidal pool (boats are available for hire), and angling from rock and beach.

The nearby **Amanzimtoti Bird Sanctuary**, Umdoni Road, is worth a visit (waterfowl are prominent; the greenbacked herons and peacocks are features; visitor facilities include bird-watching hides, a short walking trail, and cream teas at weekends). The **Ilanda Wilds Nature Reserve** is a small but beautiful and richly varied riverine haven for 160 species of bird and 120 of tree and shrub (there are nature trails and picnic spots).

NATAL SHARKS BOARD

The Natal Sharks Board has its headquarters on a hill overlooking the town, and presents fascinating demonstrations three times a week. These include the dissection of a shark, audio-visual presentations and there is a mini museum; Tue and Thu at 09:00, Wed at 11:00 and 14:30. The Board boasts the largest mould of a great white in South Africa. Demonstrations are very popular and it is advisable to book in advance, tel: (031) 561-1017.

Below: *The Natal south coast's balmy climate, its golden sands and many charming little resort centres combine to create the most enticing of holiday regions; this is Margate, one of the bigger resorts.*

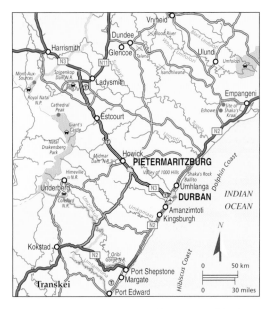

Further south of the city, the coastline is lined with scores of little towns, villages and hamlets, each with its own distinctive charm, most linked by the excellent N2 coastal highway. Prominent among these are **Scottburgh**, offering safe bathing, good fishing and Crocworld, which includes a complex of crocodile pens, a wildlife museum, a snake pit and a Zulu village where traditional dances are performed on Sunday afternoons.

Port Shepstone boasts one of the country's finest golf courses, and lively **Margate** (the hub of the so-called Hibiscus Coast and focus of annual festivals) offers beaches and a golf course, hotels and self-catering complexes, shops, restaurants and discos.

Inland from Port Shepstone is the **Oribi Gorge Nature Reserve**, a magnificent expanse of rugged hills, deep valleys, emerald grassland and a spectacular canyon; for information, contact the Natal Parks Board.

For excitement and glamour, the **Wild Coast Sun** casino resort (*see* p. 89) offers lively round-the-clock entertainment, and is only one and a half hours from Durban, and easily accessible from the South Coast Road.

NATAL MIDLANDS

The main town of the attractive region between the coastal strip and the high Drakensberg is historic and charming **Pietermaritzburg**. Beyond are the great grassland plains of central Natal, traditional home to the Zulu nation and scene of bloody 19th-century conflicts between Briton, Boer and Zulu.

DON'T MISS

** **Midmar Dam Resort** and **Nature Reserve**: well-developed area which offers swimming, fishing, boat hire and watersports, a historical village and game-viewing.
The **Pietermaritzburg** area is famed for its waterfalls. The best known are:
** **Howick**, 95 m (312 ft) high, near the town of that name; designated as a Natural Heritage site
* **Karkloof**, has picnic sites
* **Albert**, surrounded by beautiful countryside.

Pietermaritzburg ★★

A beautiful little city of red-brick Victorian buildings, cast-iron store fronts, antique shops, book stores, and of parks and gardens bright with roses and azaleas, Pietermaritzburg was founded by the Boer Voortrekkers in 1838. Its trekker origins can be seen in the **Church of the Vow**, a small, gabled edifice erected to commemorate the defeat of the Zulu army at Blood River; it now serves as a Voortrekker museum.

However, the town's history and character are British colonial rather than Afrikaner, its Victorian heritage on display in the **Macrorie House** museum and in the delightful collection of 1850s shops and houses that comprise part of the **Natal Museum** (natural history and ethnology exhibits also draw the eye). Other reminders of the past include the **Old Natal Parliament**; the magnificent **City Hall**, an imposing affair of domes, stained glass and clock tower (completed in 1900, it's the southern hemisphere's largest all-brick building); and the **Central Lanes**. This last is a network of narrow alleys that once functioned as the heart of Pietermaritzburg's financial and legal district; of interest here are the small speciality shops and the elaborate Edwardian arcade. Of special note, too, is the bronze statue of **Mohandas Gandhi**, unveiled in 1993 to com-

Right: *Pietermaritzburg City Hall is a marvellous example of the city's Victorian architectural heritage; Pietermaritzburg is renowned for its luxuriant parks and gardens filled with bright blooms.*

THE MIDLANDS MEANDER

This scenically enchanting **arts-and-crafts route** has been established north of Howick, between and around the little villages of **Nottingham Road** and **Lidgetton**. Along the route, studios and workshops offer: weaving, pottery, painting, graphics and art restoration.

The Meander is one of three routes: the **Last Outposts** and the **Natal Midlands Experience** itineraries also beckon the leisurely sightseer. Check open days with the Publicity Association in Pietermaritzburg or Howick.

Below: *The aptly named Valley of a Thousand Hills, between Pietermaritzburg and Durban.*

memorate the 'Mahatma's' arrival in South Africa 100 years ago. It stands outside the **Colonial Buildings** in the Church Street mall.

Valley of a Thousand Hills ★ ★ ★

The region's most striking physical feature is the majestic valley of the Umgeni River between the flat-topped sandstone massif of Natal Table Mountain, near Pietermaritzburg, and the Indian Ocean to the east. The area is densely populated in some parts, ruggedly wild in others; the vistas are magnificent, the flora (red-hot pokers, Mexican sunflowers, aloes and, especially, a wealth of lilies) a delight to the eye.

The road that leads along the valley's southern rim is lined with farm and craft stalls and tea gardens; there are also craft studios and shops in and around the small centre of **Bothas Hill** (among them Uncle Tom's Cabin, Selkirk's Curio Gallery, The Weavers' Studio next door, The Pottery Studio and The Barn Owl). Some intriguing African art and craft can be seen, too, in the unusual, vaguely Tudor-style **Rob Roy Hotel**, whose terrace is the venue for delicious carvery lunches and cream teas.

If you're in search of the 'authentic' Africa, make a point of visiting **PheZulu**, a 'living museum' village featuring Zulu domestic life, dancing (a pulsating spectacle), bone-throwing, African cooking, thatching, spearmaking, an art gallery and a shop. There's also Zulu dancing at nearby **Assagay Safari Park**, together with crocodiles (400 of them), snakes, a natural history museum, curio shop, colonial-style restaurant, and picnic sites.

Battlefields Route ★★

For most of the 19th century the Natal midland region was a battlefield, with Zulu, Boer and Briton fighting for territorial supremacy. Military enthusiasts – indeed anyone interested in the region's turbulent past – will find the Battlefields Route fascinating. Some of the most dramatic confrontations occurred in the triangular area bounded by Estcourt in the south, Volksrust in the north and Vryheid across to the east; among especially evocative names are Blood River, Isandhlwana, Rorke's Drift and Ulundi, Majuba Hill, Dundee, Bloukrans, Talana, Elandslaagte, Tugela Heights, Colenso, Ladysmith and Spioenkop.

Particularly notable (and very newsworthy at the time) is **Rorke's Drift**, a garrisoned mission station whose British defenders heroically resisted a massive Zulu onslaught on 1 January 1879; no less than 11 Victoria Crosses were handed out after the engagement. Worth mentioning is the **African Craft Centre** at Rorke's Drift, where you view and buy hand-woven rugs and tapestries, hand-printed fabrics and some of the finest examples of Zulu pottery. The more important battle of **Isandhlwana**, where the Zulus wiped out a far bigger British force, lies to the east.

One can either book a tour or embark on a self-guided drive around the area; call Pam McFadden, curator of the **Talana Hills Museum**, tel: (0341) 2-2654, or the local area publicity association for information (a beautifully produced selection of booklets, tapes and brochures is available). An intriguing optional extra for hire is the **Walk 'n Talk** series of tapes (audio commentary plus sound effects as you stroll around).

DRAKENSBERG ★★★

South Africa's highest mountain range is a massive and strikingly beautiful rampart of deep gorges, pinnacles and saw-edged ridges, caves, overhangs and balancing rocks. In the winter months its upper levels lie deep in snow, but clus-

Right: *The peaks and buttresses of the Drakensberg, some of which fall sheer for 2,000 m (6,565 ft), draw climbers from afar.*

tered among the foothills far below, in undulating grasslands, is a score of resort hotels, many of them old-established, unpretentious venues created and maintained for the family holiday-maker. People come for the fresh, clean mountain air; for the walks, climbs and drives; for the gentler sports (trout fishing, golf, bowls and horseback riding); and for casual relaxation in the most exquisite of surrounds. Particularly recommended are the **Northern** (the Mont-aux-Sources area) and **Central Drakensberg** (Giant's Castle to Cathedral Peak).

Royal Natal National Park ★★★

This is an extensive floral and wildlife sanctuary, home to antelope and about 200 bird species, among them the black eagle, and the bearded and Cape vultures. Also noted for its scenic magnificence and its 30 or so charted walks, one of the park's longer trails takes you up to the imposing **Mont-aux-Sources** plateau and its **Amphitheatre**; recommended is the excursion to the **Tugela Falls**, where the river plunges into the pools below in a series of cascades; one stretch drops sheer for 183 metres (600 feet), making it the country's highest waterfall. Horse-riding facilities abound throughout the Drakensberg, and numerous bridle paths cross scenically enchanting landscapes. All rides are accompanied by experienced guides. The park's streams and dams offer fine fishing.

Kosi Bay
Mont-aux-Sources
Durban
Port Edward

Left: *The Sterkspruit Falls is one of the more modest of the Drakensberg's many cataracts and cascades.*
Opposite: *The distinctive Amphitheatre, part of the Drakensberg's Mont-aux-Sources massif, and the Tugela River which plunges down to the Royal Natal National Park from a height of 3,000 m (9,855 ft).*

Accommodation is available at the Royal Natal National Park Hotel or the elegant Mont-aux-Sources Hotel nearby, as well as at the park's luxury lodge, Tendele; bungalows, cottages and camping and caravanning facilities are also available.

For reservations and further information, contact the Natal Parks Board.

Giant's Castle Game Reserve ★★★

Located farther south, in central Drakensberg, **Giant's Castle** also offers scenic splendour, horseback riding, an intriguing plant life (a large number of the Drakensberg's 800 flowering species are found here) and a superb array of birds of prey; during the harsh winter months, to assist the bearded vultures in obtaining food, they are fed at hides or 'vulture restaurants', affording visitors the opportunity to study and photograph these predatory birds at close hand.

The area is dominated by the **Giant's Castle** and **Injesuthi** buttresses; the park is famed for its wealth of Bushman rock art, some of which is on view in the two

---

THE ART OF THE ANCIENTS

The Central Drakensberg is remarkable for its caves and overhangs – rock shelters that once served as home to the long-vanished **Bushman** (or San) people, the greatest of the prehistoric artists. Prime sites are to be found in and around the massive **Ndedema Gorge**. More than 4,000 paintings are displayed in 17 cave 'galleries'. Many fine examples also survive in the **Giant's Castle** reserve to the south. Together, the two areas hold about 40% of all southern African rock art.

site museums. Accommodation is available in the Giant's Castle camp (lodges, cottages, bungalows and rustic huts) or nearby Injasuti (cabins and camp sites). Contact the Natal Parks Board for information.

NORTHERN NATAL

A region of remarkable richness and diversity, Northern Natal boasts four of South Africa's finest game reserves, and one of the world's great wetland and marine wilderness areas at Lake St Lucia, and Maputaland to the north.

Greater St Lucia Wetland Park ★★★

On and around the Zululand coast is an intricate mix of lake, lagoon, pan, marshland, papyrus swamp, sandy forest, palm veld, grassland, dune, beach and offshore coral reef, collectively known as the **Greater St Lucia Wetland Park**. Centrepiece of the huge conservation enterprise is **Lake St Lucia**, in reality an extensive, shallow and beautiful estuarine system that is home to a myriad waterfowl, and to crocodile and hippo. Giant sea turtles – endangered loggerheads and leatherbacks – use the beaches as breeding grounds. Among visitor amenities are walking trails and excellent opportunities for game-viewing, bird-watching, boating, fishing, scuba diving and snorkelling. (Don't miss the **Santa Lucia boat tour**, organized by the Natal Parks Board, which ferries visitors the length of the estuary, giving them the opportunity to see the water wildlife at close hand; the two-hour boat trip runs three times a day.) Accommodation in

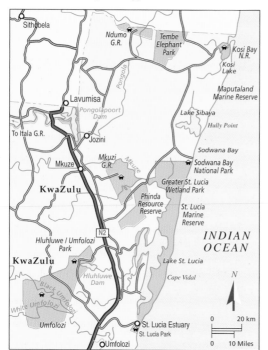

Opposite: *Three young Zulu girls, or 'intombi', wearing traditional skirts, necklaces, head- and leg-bands.*

SODWANA BAY

Northern Natal's offshore coral reefs, the most southerly in the world, are a paradise for scuba divers; especially popular are those near Sodwana Bay, an area of lake, marshland and forested sand dunes. Sodwana is also popular for deep-sea fishing, and offers excellent bird-watching and nature trails. A four-wheel drive vehicle is recommended; diving equipment can be hired. Accommodation is available at **Sodwana Bay Lodge**, tel: (031) 304-5977; the Natal Parks Board offers chalets (call central reservations) and camping facilities, tel: (035) 571-0051.

the form of hotels and hutted rest camps can be arranged through the Natal Parks Board.

Farther up the shoreline are two smaller but equally attractive stretches of water: **Lake Sibaya** (South Africa's largest freshwater lake) and **Kosi Bay** (a system of lakes, and patches of mangrove swamp, as well as palm and sycamore fig forest), close to the Mozambique border. Activities include fishing, bird-watching and walking. The ocean is popular for scuba diving and spear fishing.

Between the two lies the **Maputaland Marine Reserve** which boasts 20 different eco-systems, including three lake systems home to hippo, crocodile and a superb array of birds. Maputaland is considered to be one of the last undiscovered wilderness areas in southern Africa. Coral-encrusted reefs entice the snorkeller, and fishing is excellent from Black Rock (marlin has been caught here), a 15-minute drive from Rocktail Bay Lodge located in the reserve. For further information, contact the KwaZulu Department of Nature Conservation.

Northern Game Reserves ★★★

The Natal and Zululand game areas in the north are relatively small in size, but they are among Africa's finest:

ZULULAND

Zululand encompasses the area stretching north of the Tugela River. From one-time capital **Eshowe** to **Ulundi**, the present capital, a Zulu cultural route offers authentic *kraals* and tangible reminders of past historical battles. Inland, the Nkwaleni Valley is the location of **Shakaland**, originally created for the TV epic *Shaka Zulu*. One and a half hours from Durban, this splendid complex comprises a *kraal*-type hotel in the form of a village of beehive huts. Attractions include Zulu culinary specialities; traditional dancing; displays by *sangomas* (spirit mediums) and herbalists; basket-weaving, pot-making, hut-building; tel: (03546) 912.

Above: *Hikers on the Umfolozi wilderness trail stop to study the rugged landscape and its wildlife; the reserve is famed for its rhinos.*

the warm, humid climate and the lush countryside with its wonderful variety of grasses, shrubs and trees provide an ideal habitat for a great variety of animals and birds. The reserves offer comfortable accommodation, game-viewing roads and walking trails.

Also available are guided wilderness walks conducted by knowledgeable and competent rangers.

Among the more prominent reseerves are **Umfolozi**, and next-door **Hluhluwe** (the two are administered as a single unit and are part of the Hluhluwe–Umfolozi Park). Umfolozi is a magnificent area of woodland savanna and flood plain between the White and Black Umfolozi rivers. Famed for its rhino conservation programme, it is also a haven for the 'big five', as well as cheetah, giraffe, zebra, blue wildebeest, spotted hyena and wild dog. There are two pleasant hutted camps and two bush camps.

Hluhluwe is also strikingly beautiful. A rich compound of misty forests, grass-covered hills, dense thickets and enchanting rivers, between them they sustain 84 mammal species and an impressive 425 bird species. There are splendid accommodation facilities at Hilltop Camp, and also at Mtwazi Lodge (exclusive) as well as the Muntulu Bush Lodge.

Mkuzi is a largish sanctuary comprising savannah parkland, and riverine and sycamore fig forest to the east of the Lebombo mountains. It is renowned for its pans and water-related birdlife (and excellent viewing hides), and is also home to hippo, leopard, giraffe and antelope. Accommodation includes a hutted camp and a quite delightful bush camp.

Itala is well inland, covering an area that runs along the south bank of the Pongolo River. Its varied wildlife includes black and white rhino, buffalo, giraffe, zebra, antelope, and an array of birds. The new Ntshondwe complex, with restaurant and bar, is one of the finest public rest camps in South Africa; there are also three attractive bush camps, each of which overlooks water.

For information on any of the above reserves, contact the Natal Parks Board.

Ndumo is a smallish reserve lying on the flood plain of the Pongolo River. The river and pans sustain 400 species of avifauna, among them Pel's fishing owl and the southernbanded snake eagle. There are also hippo and crocodile, rhino, giraffe and buffalo, and the shaggy-coated nyala antelope. Accommodation is in a small, attractive hutted camp.

Tembe Elephant Park is a new reserve, created to protect the remnants of southern Mozambique's once-great elephant herds. The area is still under development; for visitors, there's one comfortable tented camp. It is advisable (and safest) to observe the elephants as part of the organized three-day group expedition.

For information on Ndumo and Tembe, call the KwaZulu Department of Nature Conservation.

PRIVATE LODGES

Private venues range from the rugged to the super-sophisticated. Located close to the wildlife areas are:
- **Phinda Resource Reserve**, near Mkuzi and Sodwana Bay: luxury lodge with sweeping views of Ubombo Mountains; superb game-viewing; one of the best ecotourism destinations.
- **Rocktail Bay**, between Kosi Bay and Sodwana: elevated reed chalets; hippos, crocodiles and flamingos.
- **Bona Manzi Game Park**, near Hluhluwe: tree-house accommodation.
- **Bushlands Game Lodge**, Hluhluwe: wooden houses on stilts.

Below: *The Mkuzi reserve's Nhlonhlela bush camp, a charming cluster of huts close to a bird-rich pan.*

Natal at a Glance

BEST TIMES TO VISIT

Winter months (**June** to **August**) balmiest time to visit the coast; tropical heat and high humidity in summer can cause discomfort. Warm Indian Ocean provides pleasant bathing, even in winter. Durban's **international airport** 15 minutes from city centre, offers full range of visitor facilities. **Bus service** operates between airport and city terminal, corner Smith and Aliwal sts.

GETTING THERE

Drakensberg
Airlink operates direct flight from Johannesburg to Pietermaritzburg's airport; Durban's airport an hour away. **Fly-in package tours** to the Drakensberg mountains, game parks and lodges can be arranged through Fly Southern African Tours, tel: (031) 562-8552. **City hopper** service runs between both airports and Pietermaritzburg.

GETTING AROUND

Car-hire firms plentiful, consult Durban Unlimited or your hotel reception for details. City **bus** and metered **taxi** services in Durban adequate (taxis cannot be hailed in street, a call needs to be placed). Excellent **Mynah minibus** shuttle service runs every 10 minutes, linking city centre with Golden Mile. **Tuk-Tuk** three-wheeled scooters useful means of transport for very short trips; make sure you determine the fare beforehand.

WHERE TO STAY

Royal Hotel, city centre: one of South Africa's oldest, best and most famous, tel: (031) 304-0331, fax: 307-6884.
Edward, Marine Parade: elegant, impeccable service, tel: (031) 37-3681, fax: 32-1692.
Elangeni, Snell Parade: opposite North Beach, tel: (031) 37-1321, fax: 32-5527.
Tropicana, Marine Parade: on bustling Pedestrian Mall, opposite Sea World, tel: (031) 368-1511, fax: 368-2322.

North Coast
Beverly Hills, Umhlanga Rocks: overlooks miles of unspoilt beaches, tel: (031) 561-2211, fax: 561-3711.
Oyster Box, Umhlanga Rocks: gracious and tranquil, tel: (031) 561-2233, fax: 561-4072.

Natal Midlands
Imperial Hotel, Pietermaritzburg: colonial style, tel: (0331) 42-6551, fax: 42-9796.
Karos Capital Towers, Pietermaritzburg: big and busy, tel: (0331) 94-2761, fax: 45-2857.
Game Valley Lodge, Crammond: luxurious wildlife getaway, tel: (03393) 787, fax: 795.
Hilton Hotel, Hilton, north of Pietermaritzburg: elegant Tudor style, tel: (0331) 3-3311, fax: 3-3722.

Wartburger Hof, Wartburg: German-style country hotel in pine-forest setting, tel/fax: (033) 503-1482.
Granny Mouse's Country House in Balgowan, half an hour from Pietermaritzburg: renowned for charming hospitality, tel/fax: (03324) 4071.

Drakensberg
Royal Natal National Park Hotel, Mont-aux-Sources: colonial-country family resort in parklike setting, tel: (036) 438-6200, fax: 438-6101.
Little Switzerland Mountain Resort, between Bergville and Harrismith: thatched cottages and self-contained chalets, tel/fax: (036) 438-6220.
Sandford Park Lodge, near Bergville: rustic, originally a coachhouse, tel: (036) 448-1001, fax: 448-1047.
Cathedral Peak Hotel, Winterton: family resort set in spectacular peaks, tel/fax: (036) 488-1888.
Drakensberg Sun, Winterton: in Cathkin Peak area, superb views, tel: (036) 468-1000, fax: 468-1224.
Sani Pass Hotel, Himeville: outstanding guest facilities, tel/fax: (033) 701-1435.
Himeville Arms, Himeville: charmingly cosy, tel: (033722), ask for 5.

Northern Natal
Bona Manzi Game Park, tel/fax: (035) 562-0181.
Bushlands Game Lodge, tel/fax (035) 562-0144.

Natal at a Glance

Phinda Resource Reserve,
tel: (011) 803-8421,
fax: 803-1810.
Rocktail Bay, tel: (011)
884-1458, fax: 883-6255.

BUDGET ACCOMMODATION
Durban City Lodge, tel:
(031) 32-1447, fax: 32-1483.
**Holiday Inn Garden
Courts**: North Beach, also
South Beach, call toll free
0800-117711.
Holiday Inn Marine Parade,
tel: (031) 37-3341,
fax: 32-9885.

WHERE TO EAT

Chatters, city centre: innovative fare in a cosy setting,
tel: (031) 306-1896.
Elarish on the Bluff: specializes in superbly spicy Indian
food, tel: (031) 466-2086.
Langoustine-by-the-Sea,
Durban North: highlights
seafood (prawn curries
are excellent), pasta also
good, tel: (031) 84-9768.
Razzmatazz: for the adventurous (porcupine kebabs,
zebra pie), tel: (031) 903-4131.
St Geran, owned by a
Mauritian: serves tasty Creole
food, tel: (031) 304-7509.
Ulundi in the Royal Hotel:
some of the best Indian food
in town, served by turbaned
waiters, tel: (031) 304-0331.

TOURS AND EXCURSIONS

Durban city
Historical walkabout:
Mon to Fri at 09:45, contact
Durban Unlimited, tel: (031)
304-4934.

Oriental walkabout: Mon to
Fri at 09:45 (visit Victoria
Street Market, Juma Mosque,
fish market), Durban Unlim-
ited, tel: (031) 304-4934.
Durban by night: city lights,
sundowners on the beach,
contact Thembani, tel:
(031) 266-8943.
Harbour tours: one-hour
boat trip out to sea on *Sarie
Marais*; regular half-hour har-
bour trips on *Harbour Maid*,
contact Durban Unlimited.
Overland and city tours
(Valley of a Thousand Hills,
Shakaland, Wild Coast Sun,
Umgeni Bird Park): U-Tours,
tel: (031) 368-2848; Intaba
Tours (in English, Dutch,
French and German), tel:
(031) 777-1405; Strelitzia
Tours (in English, French,
German, Italian and Spanish),
tel: (031) 86-1904.
Township tours (squatter
camps, Valley of a Thousand
Hills), contact Third Eye Tours,
tel: (031) 25-9645.

Drakensberg
**Mountain biking, horse rid-
ing, hiking**, tubing on
Umzimkulu River: Kwezintaba
Tours, tel: (033) 701-1017 or
a/h (033722), ask for 231.

Sani Pass tours (overnight,
plus trails, hiking, trout fishing): Molumong Tours, tel:
(033) 701-1490; Mokhotlong
Mountain Transport (day
tours), tel: (033722) ask for
1302; also Kwezintaba Tours,
tel: (033) 701-1017.

Northern Natal
Game-viewing (also bird-
watching, deep-sea fishing,
hiking and walking trails):
contact Sun Seekers Safaris,
tel: (031) 568-1647.

USEFUL CONTACTS

**Drakensberg Publicity
Association**, Hotel Walter,
Bergville, tel: (036) 448-1557.
Durban Unlimited tourist
information, 22 Gardiner St,
tel: (031) 304-4934; next to
Sea World, tel: (031) 32-2595.
**KwaZulu Department of
Nature Conservation**, 367
Loop Street, Pietermaritzburg,
tel: (0331) 94-6698.
Natal Parks Board (head-
quarters in Pietermaritzburg):
enquiries, tel: (0331)
47-1961, reservations,
tel: (0331) 47-1981.
**Pietermaritzburg Publicity
Association**, city centre, tel:
(0331) 45-1348.

DURBAN	J	F	M	A	M	J	J	A	S	O	N	D
AVERAGE TEMP. °F	76	76	75	71	66	62	62	63	66	69	72	74
AVERAGE TEMP. °C	24	25	24	22	19	17	16	17	19	20	22	23
Hours of Sun Daily	6	7	7	7	7	7	7	7	6	5	5	6
SEA TEMP. °F	75	77	75	73	70	68	66	66	68	70	72	73
SEA TEMP. °C	24	25	24	23	21	20	19	19	20	21	22	23
RAINFALL in	5	4	5	3	3	1	2	2	3	4	4	4
RAINFALL mm	135	114	124	87	64	26	44	58	65	89	104	108
Days of Rainfall	15	12	12	9	7	5	5	7	10	14	16	15

5
Eastern Cape and Transkei

This region extends along the Indian Ocean seaboard, from the seaport city of **Port Elizabeth**, along the Eastern Cape and Ciskei shorelines and the lovely Transkei Wild Coast to Natal: a varied, mostly gentle and entirely beautiful land, though one with a turbulent history. It was here that 19th-century white settler and black tribesman fought long and bitterly for territorial possession, the process of confrontation and conquest starting in earnest with the arrival in Algoa Bay of shiploads of British immigrants – 4,000 in all – in 1820.

Despite its aggressively colonial past, this is predominantly Xhosa country. Much of it is occupied by **Transkei** and **Ciskei**, traditional 'homelands' of these southern Nguni people that have, for some years, functioned as independent republics. Their return to the greater South African fold forms part of the country's transition to full democracy.

CLIMATE

The Eastern Cape straddles the transitional zone between the '**Mediterranean**' **winter** rainfall and the **subtropical summer** rainfall zones. The air becomes warmer and the summers wetter the farther north along the coast one travels.

The Transkei Wild Coast is normally 2° C (36° F) warmer than Port Elizabeth.

PORT ELIZABETH

South Africa's fifth largest city and known variously as the 'friendly city' and the 'windy city' (although it is no windier than many other coastal towns), Port Elizabeth is the economic hub of the Eastern Cape, much of the industrial activity connected with the vehicle-assembly sector. It's also a major tourist centre: set on the shores of Algoa Bay (where the 1820 British settlers landed), it numbers wide, white beaches, historic buildings, sophisticated shopping centres, and good hotels and restaurants among its drawcards.

Opposite: *The Umtamvuna River marks the boundary between Natal and the northern Transkei region.*

Opposite, below: *The lovely Donkin reserve, flanked by elegant Victorian terraced houses, lies in the heart of the city.*

Port Elizabeth has four major beaches: **King's, Humewood, Hobie** and **Pollok**. The first comprises long stretches of golden sands, boasts swimming pools, a miniature railway and an entertainment amphitheatre; the second is linked with the sheltered Happy Valley area, which offers level picnicking lawns, beyond which lie quiet lily ponds and shaded riverside paths. Colourful Hobie Beach, flanked by sociable **Shark Rock Pier**, is the scene of the action: Hobie Cat sailing, rubber-ducking and beach sports; a thriving flea market crowds the promenade above the sand at weekends. Finally, Pollok is for those who take their waves seriously.

Oceanarium and Museum Complex ★★★

A visit to Port Elizabeth's **Oceanarium** should not be missed: the dolphins, caught in the bay, are trained to play to the gallery, and Cape fur seals also get into the act, as do jackass penguins. Notable too are the Aquarium, and the **Snake Park**, one of the country's leading reptile repositories and research centres; the Reptile Rotunda hosts thematic exhibitions; the Tropical House contains colourful birds and other wildlife in a sculpted landscape of jungle-like vegetation. The **Museum**, housing the Marine Hall, the Bird Hall, the

---

JEFFREYS BAY: A SURFER'S DREAM

Less than an hour's drive along the coast west of Port Elizabeth, Jeffreys Bay is renowned for its magnificent surfing rollers (it is the venue of international competitions), for its myriad and enchanting seashells (there's a delightful display in the town's museum), and for a thriving handcraft industry.

Just south of this is St Francis Bay, whose tranquil, unspoilt beaches beckon both sun lovers and surfers.

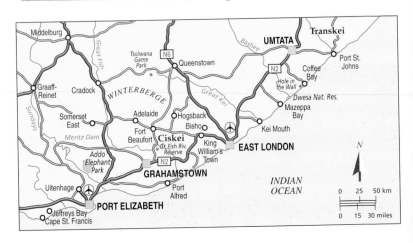

Historical Costume Gallery and a children's touch museum, is well worth an hour or two of your time.

Nature Rambles

St George's Park, a leafy area with paved walkways, has the country's oldest cricket club and bowling green, swimming baths, an art gallery, and the Victorian **Pearson Conservatory**, whose water lilies are magnificent. On the first Sunday of every month the grounds host **Art in the Park,** a large and lively craft market.

Indigenous flora and an abundance of birds flourish in **Settlers Park**, a unique green belt a stone's throw from the heart of the city, which is best enjoyed from the meandering trail through the Baakens River Gorge (it is advisable that you walk in a group).

Other unspoilt spots around Port Elizabeth offering nature walks (check entry requirements with the Publicity Association beforehand) include: **Island Conservation Area** near Sea View, 15 minutes from town, where the dense indigenous forest yields secretive bushbuck and (among 119 other bird species) the Knysna lourie, and **Van Stadens Wild Flower Reserve**, west of Port Elizabeth: its display of indigenous flowers is a delight from February to August.

Addo Elephant National Park ★★★

Just 72 kilometres (45 miles) northeast of Port Elizabeth, this reserve comprising wild bush country offers a stim-

SETTLER SAGA

Tangible evidence of Port Elizabeth's colonial heritage can be seen on the **Donkin Heritage Trail**, described in a booklet obtainable from the Publicity Association.
● **Donkin Reserve**: On his arrival in 1820, Sir Rufane Donkin, acting governor of the Cape, raised a pyramid to his late wife, Elizabeth, on a hill overlooking the bay, and renamed the settlement after her. The memorial's inscription is a touching tribute. The lighthouse built in 1861 stands beside the pyramid.
● Around **Market Square** are the City Hall, the old Public Library and St Mary's Collegiate Church (1831); nearby, the restored Railway Station and Feather Market Hall.
● **No. 7 Castle Hill** (1827), the oldest surviving settler home and one of a continuous row of attached houses on the steep hill above the city centre, houses the Historical Museum.

DON'T MISS

★★★ Oceanarium and Museum complex
★★★ Addo Elephant Park
★★ Donkin Heritage Trail, a steep, winding historical walking tour
★★ Grahamstown during the annual Arts Festival
★★ Transkei's unspoilt beaches; stay at the Wild Coast Sun
★ Experience one of the Ciskei's nature hiking trails.

MORE WILD EXPERIENCES

Zuurberg National Park, the younger sister to nearby Addo, gives visitors a contrasting experience: elephants are absent (though many antelope species, bushpig, caracal and jackal are plentiful), but guests can make the most of the birdlife and vast mountain views by walking, fishing and horse riding. A shaded guesthouse provides accommodation, reservations through the National Parks Board.

Like Addo, **Shamwari Game Reserve** is 72 km (45 miles) from Port Elizabeth. Pledged to 'conserving a way of life', this privately owned reserve on the Bushman's River is home to a variety of big game (including rhino and elephant) and birdlife. An Edwardian farmhouse, a lodge and two homes provide luxury accommodation.

ulating day trip – or longer stay. The park was proclaimed during the 1930s to preserve the remnants of the once-prolific Cape elephant. The herd, which has the same genetic make-up as the elephants of the Kruger National Park (though here only the males have tusks, which tend to be short), had been reduced to a pitiful 11 individuals, but with careful management their numbers slowly increased and now stand at around 200.

The park is also a sanctuary for black rhino, buffalo, eland, kudu and other antelope, and about 170 species of bird. Much of the area is covered by impenetrable thornbush, which makes it difficult to locate and observe the wildlife, but there are game-viewing roads and viewpoints at the water holes – the best spots from which to watch the bathing ritual, even if you have to wait. Night drives offer the resident guest the chance to see buffalo and rhino, and a selection of nocturnal creatures. It is also possible to walk the Spekboom Trail through a 400-hectare (988 acres) reserve within the park, fenced to preserve the indigenous 'valley bushveld' from elephant, buffalo and rhino. Facilities comprise self-catering chalets and an office/shop/restaurant complex.

Grahamstown's Arts Festival ★★

For an insight into 'state of the art' South African theatre, dance, music, film, fine arts and – increasingly –

Right: *Elephants in the Addo park; the wild, thickly vegetated terrain is able to support an elephant population three times denser than any other reserve in Africa.*

crafts in South Africa, make sure you don't miss the **National Festival of the Arts** held in July every year and organized by the 1820 Foundation. The venue is Grahamstown, an elegant little centre one and a half hour's drive inland from Port Elizabeth, and a focus of academic and cultural life.

Known both as the 'city of saints' for the number of its churches (40 places of worship in all) and as the 'settler city' for its British-colonial origins, Grahamstown is home to Rhodes University (one of the country's smaller but more prestigious campuses).

Focus of the festival's formal programme is the grandly modern **1820 Settlers National Monument** overlooking the town, where a multitude of venues include a 920-seat auditorium and the vast Memorial Court, whose ornamentation pays tribute to the British contribution to South Africa's cultural heritage. However, for the 10 or so days of the festival, the entire town buzzes with 'fringe' activity, which favours indigenous art and culture. Grahamstown's festival has become a major event on the country's annual social calendar.

Also worth visiting are the **Albany Museum** (which highlights a record of the settlers, but also features African artefacts), and the **Observatory Museum** (which features a rare *camera obscura*, a meridian room, and the story of diamonds).

> **STAYING FOR THE FESTIVAL**
>
> Grahamstown has three pleasant hotels, a luxury guesthouse (enquire at publicity association), and accommodation is available in private homes for the duration of the festival: call Festnest, tel: (0461) 2-9720 or Festival Homes, tel: (0461) 2-5313. In addition, private buses provide an efficient shuttle service from Port Elizabeth.

Left: *Grahamstown was one of many eastern Cape villages that started life as a frontier garrison. Characteristic of the city today are its imposing churches, among them the Anglican cathedral rising above the town square, and its beautifully preserved early settler and Victorian homes.*

DON'T MISS

*** A sundowner cruise at the Wild Coast Sun
*** A helicopter ride along the seaboard (if you're able to splash out); it's the very best way to see this stunning coast
*** The seafood – oysters, rock lobster, line fish – a speciality of the Wild Coast
* Hole-in-the-Wall: a striking natural feature south of Coffee Bay
* The excitement of a deep-sea angling trip (grunter, cob, marlin and more await) or the thrill of a catch from the rocks off the beach; most hotels offer fishing equipment for hire.

THE LAND OF THE HOBBITS

Just north of Ciskei is **Hogsback**, a magical mountain hamlet comprising a scatter of permanent homes, hotels, holiday bungalows and a shady camp site, all set above the exquisite indigenous forests that provided the inspiration for J. R. Tolkien's *The Hobbit*. A network of well-maintained paths leading alongside streams, past waterfalls and pools, and to a huge and ancient tree provides a paradise for day-walkers. At the edge of the forest you can look out over the plains with their African settlements far below, from which voices ring out clearly in the stillness.

CISKEI

South of East London (South Africa's major river port), Ciskei's coastline is similar to that of the Transkei Wild Coast (*see* opposite) but shorter – it stretches for roughly 65 kilometres (40 miles) to the Great Fish River, north of **Port Alfred** (a picturesque resort with a delightful marina and small craft harbour). The estuary of the Great Fish is distinguished by its maze of caves, tunnels and blowholes, and by its birdlife.

Inland drawcards include two notable nature reserves, of contrasting character and habitat. Largest and handiest to the coast is the **Great Fish River Reserve** complex (comprising Double Drift, Sam Knott and Andries Vosloo game reserves), home to hippo, buffalo, black rhino and many antelope species, as well as Bushman (San) rock paintings. The reserve is open to day visitors, but also offers comfortable accommodation at a restored Victorian homestead and a private camp. **Tsolwana Game Park**, a magnificent mountain reserve, incorporates a tribal resource area which earns valuable tourism revenue for the community. On view here is a wide variety of antelope and several exotic species; self-catering accommodation is offered in farmhouse lodges. Both nature reserves offer walking trails in the company of trained game guards, wildlife viewing roads, and hunting in season. Day permits for, or overnight accommodation at, either of these reserves should be pre-arranged through Contour.

TRANSKEI WILD COAST

The Transkei's shoreline is a scenic delight, an unspoilt wilderness of beaches and secluded bays, lagoons and estuaries (an impressive 18 rivers find their way to the ocean along this coastal strip), imposing cliffs and rocky reefs that probe fingerlike out to sea. Rolling green hills and patches of dense vegetation grace the hinterland.

The **Wild Coast Sun** hotel, casino and resort complex, set beside a tranquil lagoon close to Natal in the extreme north, is a prime tourist destination easily accessible from Durban; on offer is the full range of watersports and other amenities (including a superb golf course), gaming rooms, excellent restaurants, a theatre and two explosively lively show bars.

Several other resorts along this coast offer unbeatable value for the leisure-bent visitor. Prime pursuits are those you might expect to find only on an 'undiscovered' subtropical island: rock, deep-sea, surf and lagoon angling; swimming, surfing, scuba diving, lazing in the sun while dolphins frolic in the waves, and simply revelling in the unspoilt natural surroundings.

The seaboard's most distinctive physical feature is the **Hole-in-the-Wall**: a massive detached cliff, with an arched opening through which the surf thunders. A pleasant hour-and-a-half's walk south along the coast from **Coffee Bay** (or an hour's drive – there is no coastal road) will bring you to it.

Transkei's coastal conservation areas are the small adjoining **Dwesa** and **Cwebe nature reserves,** whose attractions include birds, antelope, winding rivers, evergreen forest and a waterfall; accommodation is available (chalets and bungalows). Book with the Department of Agriculture and Forestry.

Opposite: *A typical Xhosa homestead in rural Transkei. The Xhosa women are renowned for the beauty and variety of their beadwork.* **Below:** *The Hole-in-the-Wall on Transkei's Wild Coast is a spectacular detached cliff through which the waves relentlessly pound.*

Eastern Cape and Transkei at a Glance

BEST TIMES TO VISIT

Port Elizabeth
Mid-January to **May**; days are warm and almost windless.
Ciskei
September to **February** (summer); however, when it snows in winter, the mountains are beautiful.
Transkei
April to **August** (winter): light breezes and low humidity ensure perfect days, and accommodation rates are low.

GETTING THERE

Port Elizabeth's **airport** is 4 km (2 miles) from the city; serviced by SAA. Taxi, hotel transport and car hire services available.

Ciskei
Closest airport is East London, serviced by SAA. **Hotel transfers** available from airport.

Tourists can make use of the **bus service** run by Intercape Ferreira Coaches between East London and Port Elizabeth: it stops off at the Mpekweni and Fish River Sun resorts along the way, tel: (021) 934-4400.

Transkei
Entry requirements
All non-South African citizens must present passport and visa (purchasable on the spot or at Transkei consulates) at border posts – while these still exist.

The best way to get to the Wild Coast resorts is to **fly in**. Transkei Airways offer packages from Johannesburg to Umtata's airport; also from Durban with **helicopter connection** between Umtata and coast, tel: (011) 394-1834 (Johannesburg) or (031) 42-5738 (Durban).

Airlink also flies to Umtata from Durban, East London and Port Elizabeth, tel: (041) 51-2310.

Several major resorts have their own airstrips. The best advice is to discuss travel arrangements with your hotel, as driving is not recommended: coastal roads are narrow, often potholed; there are blind rises and sharp bends, and pedestrians and livestock are a continual hazard. If you do travel by car, make sure you lock up valuables or take them with you.

GETTING AROUND

Port Elizabeth
Circle Bus runs between Main Street and Hill shopping areas during peak hours on weekdays.

Ciskei and Transkei
Most resorts offer varied activities centred on the hotel complex, so guests normally don't stray far from their holiday base; otherwise enquire at hotel reception.

WHERE TO STAY

Port Elizabeth
Beach Hotel: close to Oceanarium and colourful Hobie Beach, tel/fax: (041) 53-2161.

Edward Hotel, opposite Donkin Memorial: newly renovated, Edwardian style with traditional service, tel/fax: (041) 56-2056.
Walmer Gardens Hotel: set in leafy suburb with restful country atmosphere, tel/fax: (041) 51-4322.
Marine Protea: situated on Summerstrand beachfront, specializes in seafood, tel/fax: (041) 53-2101.
Jeffreys Bay Holiday Resort: self-catering units with views of sea, within walking distance of main beach, tel: (04231) 3-1330.

BUDGET ACCOMMODATION
Port Elizabeth
City Lodge, Summerstrand, tel: (041) 56-3322, fax: 56-3374.
Holiday Inn Garden Court, King's Beach, tel: (041) 52-3720, fax: 55-5754.

NATURE RESERVES
Port Elizabeth
Addo Elephant National Park: self-contained cottages and thatched rondavels, camping facilities, tel: (0425) 40-0556, fax: 40-0196.
Shamwari Game Reserve: Long Lee Manor (a luxurious Edwardian mansion), Shamwari Lodge (rustic safari decor), and two renovated settler homes, tel: (042) 851-1196, fax: 31-1391.
Zuurberg National Park: Kabouga Guesthouse with lapa and swimming dam, tel: (0426) 40-0581.

Eastern Cape and Transkei at a Glance

Ciskei
(For bookings at the following reserves, call Contour, tel: (0401) 95-2115, fax: 9-2756.)
Tsolwana Game Park: high-ceilinged farm-house lodges (both self- and full-catering options available).
Great Fish River Reserve: restored Victorian homestead, and stone-and-thatch lodges with river views.

Transkei
(To book at the following reserves, contact Department of Agriculture & Forestry, Private Bag Umtata, tel: (0471) 2-4322 or 24-9309.)
The Haven Hotel, Cwebe Nature Reserve: thatched bungalows in tropical gardens, close to beach.
Dwesa Nature Reserve: wooden chalets on stilts set in lush environment, with views of forest or sea.

Hogsback
Hogsback Inn, tel: (045642), ask for 6.
King's Lodge, tel: (045642), ask for 24, fax: ask for 58.

Coastal Resorts
Ciskei
Fish River Sun hotel and casino east of Port Alfred: excellent facilities, magnificent golf course, tel: (0405) 66-1101, fax: 66-1115.
Mpekweni Sun marine resort: broad beach and lagoon, hiking trails, tel: (0431) 5-8003, fax: 66-1040.

Transkei
Wild Coast Sun: tropical island hotel and casino, Sun International central reservations, tel: (011) 780-7800. (For bookings at the following resorts, call Wild Coast Hotels central reservations, tel: (0471) 2-5344/5/6, fax: 2-3548.)
Kob Inn, Qolora Mouth: cottage-style bungalows, excellent fishing.
Trennery's Hotel: thatched bungalows, the 'country club' of the region.
Seagulls Beach Hotel: beachfront hideaway, good recreational facilities.
Mazeppa Bay Hotel: rooms and rondavels, great fishing.

Where to Eat
Port Elizabeth
A Stone's Throw, Cape Recife: island-style setting for tapas at the sea, tel: (041) 53-3546.
Cadillac Jacks: trendy with Hollywood-style jukebox, tel: (041) 53-4408.
No 49 Havelock St: restored 1859 building, menu changes daily, tel: (041) 56-4949.
Sir Rufane Donkin Rooms: interleading rooms crammed with fascinating memorabilia, tel: (041) 55-5534.
The Lemon Tree: indoor/outdoor setting filled with exquisite roses, tel: (041) 56-4782.

Ciskei and Transkei
All hotels have their own restaurant facilities.

Tours and Excursions
City day tours, tailormade tours, Algoa Tours, tel: (041) 51-2403.
Harbour cruises (day and evening) in Port Elizabeth, Nauticat, tel: (041) 55-3089.
Hiking and nature trails through the Ciskei, Contour, tel: (0401) 95-2115.
Mountain tours, also trips to Ciskei game and nature reserves, Tour and Trail, tel: (041) 52-2042.

Useful Contacts
Contour (Ciskei Tourism Board), tel: (0401) 95-2115.
National Parks Board, tel: (012) 343-1991.
Port Elizabeth Publicity Association, tel: (041) 52-1315.
Transkei Tourism Board, tel: (0471) 2-6685.

PORT ELIZABETH	J	F	M	A	M	J	J	A	S	O	N	D
AVERAGE TEMP. °F	70	70	69	65	61	58	57	57	60	62	65	68
AVERAGE TEMP. °C	21	21	20	18	16	14	14	14	15	17	18	20
Hours of Sun Daily	9	8	7	7	7	7	7	8	7	8	9	7
SEA TEMP. °F	70	70	68	66	63	61	61	61	63	64	66	70
SEA TEMP. °C	21	21	20	19	17	16	16	16	17	18	19	21
RAINFALL in	2	2	2	2	3	2	2	3	3	2	2	1
RAINFALL mm	41	39	55	57	68	61	54	75	70	59	49	34
Days of Rainfall	2	8	10	9	9	8	8	10	9	11	11	9

6
Garden Route

The southern Cape's coastal terrace, which runs from **Storms River** and the **Tsitsikamma** area in the east to **Mossel Bay** in the west is an enchanting shoreline of lovely bays, high cliffs and wide estuaries with a hinterland of mountains, spectacular passes, rivers, waterfalls and wooded ravines, while the lagoons and lakes around **Knysna** and **Wilderness** are magical stretches of water.

The attractions are many: good hotels and eating places; pleasant villages, resorts and marinas; and a warm ocean that beckons bather, yachtsman and angler.

Farther inland is Oudtshoorn and the Little Karoo, a region that has its own special fascination.

CLIMATE

The Garden Route's climate is **equable** throughout the year: it has plenty of **sunshine**, with only modest extremes of heat and cold. **Winter** nights can be very cold in the upper reaches; **snow** often covers the heights. In **summer**, strong winds sporadically assault the coastal areas and it can be very humid, but for the most part the days are **sunfilled** and **balmy**.

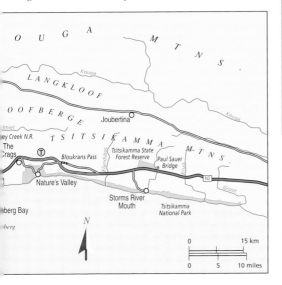

Opposite: *The shores of the Tsitsikamma National Park, a magnificent strip of coastal plateau rich in plants. The famed Otter Trail winds its way through the park.*

Right: *The resort centre at the mouth of the Storms River which rises in the Tsitsikamma mountains.*
Opposite: *The information centre in the Tsitsikamma forest reserve; among the trees are giant yellowwoods.*

DON'T MISS

*** Tsitsikamma National Park plus a night at Storms River Mouth
*** A stroll along Plettenberg Bay's unspoilt beaches
*** A visit to Knysna Heads
** A scenic ride on the Outeniqua Choo-tjoe
** A trip to Oudtshoorn, land of the ostrich barons, and the Cango Caves.

TRAIN IT

The **Outeniqua Choo-tjoe** is a Class 24 narrow-gauge steam train that plies between **George** and **Knysna**, crossing the spectacular Kaaimans River bridge to run through lovely wooded country, along the shoreline and over the lagoon. The journey takes just over three hours, and you have time to enjoy a pub lunch before the return trip (excursions Mon to Fri, and Sat during Christmas school holidays). Bookings may be made at George railway station or tel: (0441) 73-8202; or contact the local tourism office, tel: (0441) 74-4000.

COASTAL TERRACE
Tsitsikamma Area

The **Tsitsikamma National Park** embraces an 80-kilometre-strip (50 miles) of superb coastline together with a marine reserve that stretches five kilometres (three miles) offshore. The land area is richly endowed with plant life and birds; the rock pools teem with colourful marine life; and whales and dolphins can often be seen sporting close to the shoreline. The forest reserve's indigenous trees include the giant yellow-woods, which can grow to over 50 metres (165 feet); among these is the famous 'Big Tree', estimated to be over 800 years old. Within the park there are various nature walks winding through beautiful forests and along the scenic cliffs. For adventurous swimmers and divers, there is an underwater trail.

The park is also traversed by the popular five-day **Otter Hiking Trail**, which leads through 41 kilometres (25 miles) of unsurpassed coastal scenery from **Storms River Mouth** to **Nature's Valley**, a charming village in a setting of mountain, forest, lagoon and sea.

Visitors to the Tsitsikamma area are recommended to spend a night in the fully equipped oceanettes, cottages or chalets at the Storms River Mouth rest camp (the beautiful surrounds make this a popular stopover). For more information contact the National Parks Board.

Plettenberg Bay

One of South Africa's most fashionable resort centres, its bay, unspoilt beaches and surrounds are a scenic delight. Plettenberg Bay's amenities include country inns, holiday cottages, restaurants, discos, some very inviting shops, boutiques and bars, and **Beacon Island**, which supports a large and sophisticated hotel and time-share complex; and there are facilities for golf, bowls, horse riding, angling, scuba diving, boating and sailing.

The nearby **Robberg** and **Keurbooms River** nature reserves attract ramblers and bird-watchers.

Recommended picnic excursions include those to the **Kranshoek** lookout point and picnic site, part of the Harkerville State Forest, and to the **Garden of Eden**, where many of the trees are labelled.

> ### WHAT TO SEE AND DO IN KNYSNA
>
> • **Millwood Museum**: displays of local history, gold mining, timber industry.
> • Try fresh oysters at Knysna Oyster Co. or lunch at Jetty Tapas on **Thesen's Island**.
> • Visit the Norman-style church and historic guest-house at **Belvidere**.
> • Stroll past the five **castles** on the sea at **Noetzie** (note, these are private residences).
> • Enjoy the art and crafts at **Die Ou Fabriek**, in the garden of Craft House. Also **Bitou Crafts**: spinners, weavers and knitters at work.

Knysna

Knysna, also a popular resort centre, is celebrated for its excellent locally brewed draught ale (Mitchell's), its fresh oysters and fine furniture made from the area's hardwoods. The biggest drawcard is **Knysna Lagoon**, a magnificent stretch of water guarded by two imposing sandstone cliffs known as **The Heads**.

The lagoon, popular among boating enthusiasts, water-skiers and fishermen, harbours an astounding variety of fish and birds, crabs, prawns, 'pansy shells' and the very rare sea horse (*Hippocampus capensis*). Cabin cruisers and houseboats can be hired; the **John Benn**, a handsome 20-ton pleasure boat, leaves from the jetty each morning (sightseeing, live entertainment, wining and dining on board); booking is essential.

You get a fine view of Knysna, its lagoon and of **Leisure Island** (an attractive, largely residential development) from the eastern Head; on the western one is the **Featherbed Nature Reserve**, which is open to the public. Access to the reserve is by boat (at no extra charge). Guided excursions are on offer along the lovely **Bushbuck Walk**; gourmet meals can be enjoyed in the forest restaurant.

Knysna Forest, together with the Tsitsikamma woodlands to the east, form South Africa's largest expanse of indigenous high forest: a 36,400-hectare (89,940 acres) home to giant yellowwood, stinkwood and other indigenous trees, and haven to the last four survivors of the region's Cape bush elephant. The **Diepwalle Forest Station**, off the R339, is the starting point for the **Elephant Walk**, some 20 kilometres (12 miles) in total (there are shorter routes) through this impressive forest.

Wilderness Lakes Area

Wilderness is an enchanting little seaside resort centre to the west of Knysna, set around a lagoon which is the first in a chain of 'lakes' that lie between the two towns.

The wider area, administered by the National Parks Board, embraces five rivers, 28 kilometres (17 miles) of coastline and six large bodies of water: the **Wilderness Lagoon**, the **Serpentine**, **Island Lake**, **Langvlei**, **Rondevlei** and **Swartvlei**. A wealth of aquatic plants, and the sedge and reed beds provide food and shelter for fish and for about 200 species of bird, including 80 different types of waterfowl.

The Wilderness area is very popular among holidaymakers; Swartvlei and Eilandvlei are favoured by water sportsmen, and the whole region by ramblers, hikers, bird-watchers and anglers. Rondevlei and Langvlei – where you can see fish eagles, ospreys, herons and kingfishers – both have bird hides. Accommodation is available in several good hotels, holiday cottages and National Parks Board chalets.

Mossel Bay

Since the discovery and exploitation of offshore oil deposits, Mossel Bay has grown considerably, but it nevertheless remains a popular holiday destination for many.

Below: *Sandstone 'heads' flank the sea entrance to Knysna's lovely lagoon.*

In prehistoric times the area was home to the Khoikhoi 'Strandlopers' (beach walkers), whose staple diet of mussels gave the bay its name. It was also known to the earliest of the European seafarers: in 1501 the Portuguese admiral João da Nova built a small stone chapel on the shores (nothing remains of this); Bartolomeu Dias, Vasco da Gama and others filled their ships' casks from the perennial spring and 'posted' letters and documents in the trunk of a large milkwood tree for collection by the next passing fleet. Something of this intriguing past can be seen in the town's **Bartolomeu Dias Museum**.

Also of interest to visitors is **Seal Island**, which is home to around 2,000 of these marine mammals (cruises start from the harbour), and **The Point**, from which you get spectacular seascape views (whales and dolphins can sometimes be seen).

THE LITTLE KAROO

This distinctive, and in places beautiful, region sprawls between the **Outeniqua** and **Langeberg** mountain ranges and the grand **Swartberg**. The flattish plain below these uplands is part of the Karoo system, but is very different from the Great Karoo wilderness that lies beyond the Swartberg. It doesn't get much rain, but good water is available from the many streams that flow down from the mountains, and the land yields rich harvests of wheat and emerald-green lucerne, tobacco, grapes and walnuts.

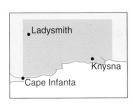

SCENIC MOUNTAIN PASSES

Several scenic and historic roads lead off the Garden Route to cross the various mountain ranges. Among the most impressive is the **Swartberg Pass**, 24 km (15 miles) of stunning views between Oudtshoorn and Prince Albert, on the fringes of the Great Karoo. Equally attractive are the **Bloukrans** and the **Grootrivier passes**, in the Tsitsikamma area; **Prince Alfred's Pass** between Knysna and the Longkloof; **Montagu Pass** between George and Herolds Bay; the **Outeniqua Pass** between George and Oudtshoorn; **Robinson Pass** between Mossel Bay and Oudtshoorn; **Garcia's Pass** between Riversdale and Ladismith in the Little Karoo; and **Seweweekspoort** (Seven Weeks Pass) described as being 'among the scenic wonders of the world' – through the Swartberg.

Left: *The 'Outeniqua Choo-Tjoe', an old steam train, offers tourists an especially scenic excursion between Knysna and George.*

Oudtshoorn

The Little Karoo's main town, set on the banks of the Grobbelaars River, was (and still is) the focal point of the ostrich industry, which had its heyday during the fashion-led ostrich-feather boom in the late 19th and early 20th centuries. Reminders of this time can still be seen in one or two ostentatious 'feather palaces', built by the wealthy farmers and traders of yesteryear.

Visit the annex of the **C. P. Nel Museum** for its Ostrich Room, and its collections of antiques and old firearms. Other surviving mansions include **Dorphuis**, **Pinehurst** and, outside town, **Greystones** and **Welgeluk** (on the Safari ranch property, *see* below).

Among the ostrich show-farms are the worthwhile **Highgate,** and **Safari**. Both offer guided tours during which you are shown all facets of the ostrich business, and you are given the opportunity to watch the birds going through their paces on the racetrack (these are known as 'ostrich derbys').

If you are adventurous enough, you can even choose to ride astride one yourself.

Below: *The riding of ostriches is cause for much hilarity among visitors to Oudtshoorn's show-farms.*

For a briefer visit, call in at the **Cango Ostrich Farm**, where the tour is quicker and more intensive.

Visitors in more leisurely mode can take the **Ostrich Express** through the Little Karoo to Calitzdorp; you're shown around a wine estate, treated to dinner and entertainment and then returned by rail the next morning.

Above: *An illuminated chamber in the giant Cango Caves; not all the labyrinths have been charted.*

Cango Caves ★★★

This labyrinthine complex of caverns, in the Swartberg range some 25 kilometres (16 miles) north of Oudtshoorn, is ranked among the most remarkable of Africa's natural wonders. The 28 chambers of Cango One (the first of the sequences to be charted) are linked by over two kilometres (one mile) of passages, and contain a marvellous fantasia of weirdly sculpted, many-coloured stalagmites and stalactites. It takes about two hours to walk this route, but elderly people, or those who are a little less energetic, need not complete the full tour.

Biggest of the caves is the Grand Hall, 16 metres (53 feet) high and 107 metres (350 feet) across. Among the more interesting dripstone formations are those with names like 'Organ Pipes', 'Cleopatra's Needle' and the 'Frozen Waterfall'.

The caves are open daily; there are conducted tours (every hour on the hour in peak season, every two hours at other times), a restaurant and a curio shop.

CANGO CROCODILE RANCH AND CHEETAHLAND

Situated 3 km (2 miles) from Oudtshoorn, on the way to the Cango Caves, this farm has over **400 crocodiles** and **American alligators**, as well as a unique complex where Africa's largest cats can be observed in their natural environment. A raised walkway through natural bushveld allows visitors to watch and photograph **cheetah, lion** and **jaguar**. The walkway ends in a bird park with a water cascade. Open daily all year round from 08:00. Guided tours are conducted every half-hour during school holidays, otherwise hourly, tel: (0443) 22-5593, fax: (0443) 22-4167.

Garden Route at a Glance

BEST TIMES TO VISIT

A mild, equitable climate makes it a pleasant destination all year round. Highest rainfall (though not excessive) in **August** and **September** (late winter). Busiest during **December** school holidays.

GETTING THERE

The Garden Route's main **airport** is 10 km (6 miles) from George. Regular flights by SAA from South Africa's major cities. **Grace Express Shuttle** travels between airport and Garden Route's major centres three times a day, tel: (0445) 82-5403 for more information.

GETTING AROUND

An excellent **network of roads** links the main towns of the Garden Route.

Tourists can make use of Intercape Ferreira Coaches, tel: (021) 934-4400, and Translux Coach Express, tel: (021) 405-3333, to travel between any of the Garden Route's main centres. Contact the **coach service** directly or ask at any travel agent.

Major **car-hire** firms represented at the airport and in the area.

WHERE TO STAY

Tsitsikamma

Forest Hall, The Crags: built in 1864, nestled in the forest, tel/fax: (04457) 8869.

Tsitsikamma Forest Inn, Storms River: set in the foothills, lovely views, tel: (042) 541-1711, fax: 541-1669.

Storms River Mouth rest camps in Tsitsikamma National Park, sea views, forest atmosphere, contact local National Parks Board, tel: (042) 541-1607.

Plettenberg Bay

Beacon Island Hotel: unique setting at the sea's edge, both time-share and hotel facilities, tel: (04457) 3-1120, fax: 3-3880.

The Plettenberg: elegant, international reputation, perched on a cliff with great sea views, tel: (04457) 3-2030, fax: 3-2074.

Hunter's Country House: exclusive thatched retreat overlooking indigenous forests, beautifully decorated rooms, tel: (04457) 7818, fax: 7878.

Wilderness

Fairy Knowe Hotel: quaint thatched rondavels and riverside rooms, wide range of watersports, tel: (0441) 9-1100, fax: 9-0563.

Karos Wilderness Hotel: renowned for its quality, sandwiched between forest and sea, tel: (0441) 9-1110, fax: 9-0600.

Far Hills Protea: country hotel at the foothills of the Outeniqua Mountains, call toll free 0800-119000.

Knysna

Belvidere House: lovingly restored historic home at lagoon edge, tel: (0445) 87-1055, fax: 87-1059.

Old Drift Forest Lodges: self-catering log chalets tucked among trees on the banks of Knysna River, tel/fax: (0445) 2-1994.

Lake Pleasant Hotel, Sedgefield: set in nature reserve, on lake's banks, tel: (04455) 3-1313, fax: 3-2040.

Under Milkwood: stylish self-catering timber chalets, nestled among milkwood trees, at Knysna Lagoon's edge, tel: (0445) 2-2385, fax: 2-2494.

Mossel Bay

Eight Bells Mountain Inn, at the foot of Robinson Pass: mountain setting, horse riding and walking trails, tel/fax: (0444) 95-1544.

Old Post Office Tree Guest House: part of historic, stone museum complex at site of ancient milkwood tree where Portuguese navigators left messages 500 years ago, tel: (0444) 91-3738, fax: 91-3104.

Santos Protea: gracious hotel overlooking Santos Beach, watersports haven, call toll free 0800-119000, fax: (0444) 91-1945.

George

Fancourt Hotel and Country Club Estate: elegant and stylish, set against the Outeniqua Mountains, stunning golf course for exclusive use of hotel guests, tel: (0441) 70-8282, fax: 70-7605.

Garden Route at a Glance

Hoogekraal Country Inn: gracious homestead dating back to 18th century, close to unspoilt beaches, tel: (0441) 79-1277, fax: 79-1300.

Oudtshoorn
Kango Protea: charming thatched rondavels in farm-like setting, tel: (0443) 22-6161, fax: 22-6772.
Rosenhof Country Lodge: restored Victorian house, country cuisine, herb and rose-filled gardens, tel: (0443) 22-2232, fax: 22-2260.

BUDGET ACCOMMODATION
Holiday Inn Garden Courts: Wilderness, tel: (0441) 9-1104, fax: 9-1134. Oudtshoorn, tel: (0443) 22-2201, fax: 22-3003.

WHERE TO EAT

Plettenberg Bay
Lud's Island: seafood specialities in privately owned estuary island hotel, tel: (04457) 9442.
Stromboli's: between Knysna and Plettenberg Bay: fine country dining, tel: (04457) 7760.
The Islander, 8 km (5 miles) outside Plettenberg Bay in Harkerville: tropical island setting, enormous seafood buffet, booking essential, tel: (04457) 7776.

Knysna
Crab's Creek Waterfront Tavern: restored house with Tudor-style timbered ceilings, tel: (0445) 87-1043.

Featherbed Tavern, Featherbed Nature Reserve: recent winner of oyster cooking competition; open-fire fish braais, tel: (0445) 81-0590.
Jetty Tapas: Spanish-style seafood buffet right on water's edge, very popular; locally brewed Mitchell's beer on offer, tel: (0445) 2-1927.
Pink Umbrella on Leisure Island: open-air, deliciously healthy eating under the milkwood trees, tel: (0445) 2-2409.

Mossel Bay
The Gannet, museum complex: specializes in fresh oysters, mussels and line fish, tel: (0444) 3738.
The Post Tree: charming stone building, the finest seafood, tel: (0444) 4402.

George
The Copper Pot: elegant dining, tel: (0441) 74-3191.
The Wine Barrel: very good home cooking, tel: (0441) 73-4370.

TOURS AND EXCURSIONS

Golf the Garden Route, Why Not Travel, tel: (04457) 3-2873.

Houseboats for hire, also one-hour trips and sunset cruises, Lightley's Holiday Cruisers, tel: (0445) 87-1026.
John Benn boat trips for elegant wining and dining, tel: (0445) 2-1693.
Tailormade Tours, Springbok Atlas, tel: (0441) 70-7993; Abba Tours (for smaller groups), tel: (0441) 74-1903; Sam's Tours, tel: (0441) 74-2100, page code 1957.
Walking and hiking tours, Why Not Travel, tel: (04457) 3-2873.

USEFUL CONTACTS

George Tourist Office, York St, tel: (0441) 74-4000.
Knysna Publicity Association, 40 Main Road, tel: (0445) 2-1610.
Mossel Bay Publicity Association, Church St, tel: (0444) 91-2202.
National Parks Board: head office, tel: (012) 343-1991; Storms River Mouth, tel: (042) 541-1607.
Oudtshoorn Publicity Association, Baron van Reede and Voortrekker sts, tel: (0443) 22-2221, fax (0443) 22-5007.

MOSSEL BAY	J	F	M	A	M	J	J	A	S	O	N	D
AVERAGE TEMP. °F	70	70	68	64	63	61	59	59	60	62	64	68
AVERAGE TEMP. °C	21	21	20	18	17	16	15	15	15	16	18	20
Hours of Sun Daily	7	7	7	7	8	8	8	7	7	7	7	7
SEA TEMP. °F	72	72	68	66	64	61	61	61	61	62	66	70
SEA TEMP. °C	22	22	20	19	18	16	16	16	16	17	19	21
RAINFALL in	1	1	1.5	1.5	1.5	1	1	1.5	1.5	1.5	1	1
RAINFALL mm	28	31	36	40	37	31	32	36	39	38	34	28
Days of Rainfall	7	7	8	8	8	7	7	8	8	9	8	6

7

Cape Town and Surrounds

Cape Town's metropolis huddles in the 'bowl' formed by majestic **Table Mountain**, its flanking peaks and the broad sweep of **Table Bay**. Suburbs and satellite towns sprawl across the low-lying **Cape Flats** and southwards over much of the scenically beautiful **Cape Peninsula**. Inland are the grand mountain ranges and fertile valleys of the Cape winelands, contrasting with the rugged, windswept West Coast (having its own special beauty) and, beyond, bleak **Namaqualand**, which is transformed in spring with vast, sweeping fields of brilliantly coloured wildflowers.

South Africa's oldest city, Cape Town was founded by the first Dutch settlers who, led by Jan van Riebeeck, landed on the tip of Africa in April 1652. Set beneath the grandeur of Table Mountain, the area was described by English circumnavigator Francis Drake as 'the fairest Cape in all the circumference of the earth', though later, as a busy and hospitable port on the sea route to India, the town earned the name 'tavern of the seas'.

The harbour is quieter than it was in the heyday of the great Union Castle passenger liners, but a part of the waterfront has been imaginatively redeveloped for tourism, plenty of ships still call, and marine and mercantile industries contribute a lot to the local economy.

Among the top attractions are a myriad eating and drinking places, excellent hotels, craft markets and speciality shops, a lively calendar of arts, superb beaches, Kirstenbosch Botanical Gardens, Table Mountain and the Peninsula's scenic hills and splendid coastline.

CLIMATE

The Southwestern Cape has a **Mediterranean** climate, receiving winter rainfall. The **long summer days** are sometimes perfect in their stillness, but they're more often disturbed by a gusty **southeaster** (known as the 'Cape doctor' because it clears away the city smog) that may last for days and can reach gale force. **Winter** is **wet** and **cool** (snow sometimes falls on the inland mountains). It is wise, even in summer, to bring warm clothes and a waterproof jacket.

Opposite: *The unmistakable shape of Table Mountain, viewed from Milnerton. The massif on the right is Lion's Head.*

Opposite: *Table Mountain viewed from Signal Hill.*

CAPE TOWN
Table Mountain ★★★

This is Cape Town's premier attraction. The mountain rises 1,086 metres (3,564 feet) above sea level and there are magnificent views from its distinctively flat-topped summit. Often, though, the heights are mantled by clouds that billow over its rim and tumble over its precipitous northern faces in a continuous and spectacular process known as the 'tablecloth'. At the top there are short walks, a licensed restaurant and a souvenir shop.

You can reach the summit on foot along one of several charted paths; some are easy, others difficult – and the mountain, despite warnings, regularly takes its toll of human life. Arm yourself with a good map or climb with someone who knows the way. Take warm clothing with you: what starts as a warm, sunny day can, and often does, change to mist and bitter chill within minutes.

Most visitors make the ascent by **cable car**. The five-minute trip is absolutely safe (there hasn't been a serious

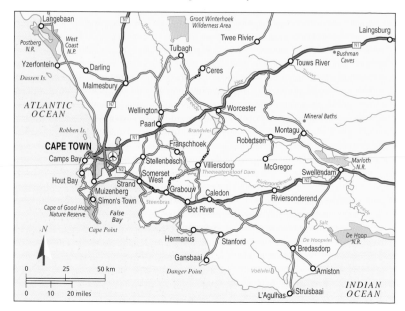

accident in over 50 years) and operates all year round (subject to weather conditions) between 08:00 and 22:00 from December to April, 08:30 and 18:00 from May to November. The nicest time for this trip is during the late afternoon, to catch the sunset; take along a picnic. During peak season you may wait for hours if you stand in line for a place; rather book in advance, tel: (021) 24-5148.

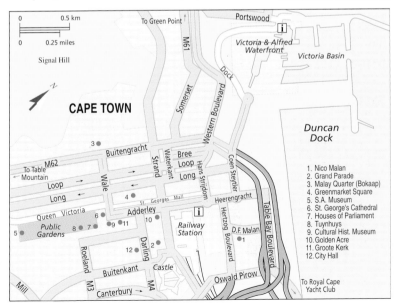

1. Nico Malan
2. Grand Parade
3. Malay Quarter (Bokaap)
4. Greenmarket Square
5. S.A. Museum
6. St. George's Cathedral
7. Houses of Parliament
8. Tuynhuys
9. Cultural Hist. Museum
10. Golden Acre
11. Groote Kerk
12. City Hall

Overlooking the city's **Grand Parade**, the Castle is the oldest occupied building in South Africa: the massive pentagonal fortress was designed to defend the fledgling Dutch colony against assault from both land and sea, and was completed in 1676. Today the Castle serves primarily as a museum; on display are furniture, carpets, objets d'art and some of the best paintings of the noted **William Fehr Collection**. There's also an array of military and period artefacts. It's open to the public daily from 10:00 to 16:00, and guided tours are offered at 10:00, 11:00, 12:00, 14:00 and 15:00, tel: (021) 408-7911.

Above: *The Heerengracht thoroughfare is part of the Foreshore, a flat expanse of land that was reclaimed from the sea.*

Central Cape Town ★

This is one of the few South African centres that is best explored on foot. A pleasant walk could start in **Adderley Street**, the city's main thoroughfare. Making your way towards the mountain, the huge, glitzy **Golden Acre** complex of stores, speciality shops, cinemas and eating places is on the left, as are the flower market, where one can bargain for exquisite blooms with the good-humoured stall-holders; the **Dutch Reformed Groote Kerk**, noted for its fine woodwork; and the **Cultural History Museum**, originally the local slave lodge and brothel and now containing some fascinating displays.

At the top of Adderley Street is **St George's Cathedral**, which offers some fine stained-glass work, an angelic choir and, occasionally, a sermon by Nobel laureate Archbishop Desmond Tutu. Turn into **St George's Mall**, a nine-block, brick-paved pedestrian walkway lined with shops and arcades and enlivened by umbrella-shaded bistros and buskers. Pleasant digressions are the cobblestoned **Greenmarket Square**, one of Africa's prettiest plazas and usually filled to capacity with market stalls, and then on to fascinating Long Street. Once the vibrant centre of city life, this street is now rather seedy but it has a few good antique and book shops (Clarkes' reputation extends well beyond the city's bounds), two mosques, the elegant **Sendinggestig** church museum and some enchantingly filigreed Victorian and Edwardian buildings.

The Public Gardens ★★

Formally known as **The Company's Garden** (it began life in the 1650s as Jan van Riebeeck's humble vegetable patch), this refreshing expanse of greenery lies beyond St

George's Cathedral. It's a must for anyone interested in plants: more than 8,000 different kinds of tree, shrub and flower – most of exotic origin – can be seen in the beautifully laid-out and maintained grounds. Running along the Gardens' eastern boundary is an oak-lined walkway known as **Government Avenue**, with benches for those who like to linger a while in the dappled shade. At the mountain end is an aviary and a shady tea garden (don't expect too much in the way of food and service, but the setting is lovely).

To beckon the stroller, notable buildings around Government Avenue are the handsome **Houses of Parliament** and Colonial Regency-style **Tuynhuis** (the state president's town residence); the **National Gallery**, which contains around 7,000 works of art; the domed and twin-towered **Great Synagogue** and its next-door neighbour, the **Old Synagogue**, housing the treasures of the Jewish Museum; the **South African Museum**, whose Karoo fossils and Bushman exhibits are special, and the adjacent **Planetarium**; and the **South African Library**, one of the world's first free libraries, which periodically stages intriguing thematic exhibitions (local history, rare Africana and so forth).

MUSEUMS AND GALLERIES

Koopmans-De Wet House, city centre: furniture, ceramics, etc.
Michaelis Collection (Old Town House), Greenmarket Square: 17th-century Dutch and Flemish paintings
Natale Labia Museum, Muizenberg: fine furniture and works of art
Rhodes Cottage, between Muizenberg and St James: Cecil Rhodes' last home; contains personal relics
Simon's Town Museum and nearby **Martello Tower**: interesting naval and local history exhibits.

PICK OF THE WATERFRONT RESTAURANTS

• **Bertie's Landing**: seafood on the quayside while seals roll in the water
• **Morton's on the Wharf**: New Orleans-inspired, Creole and spicy Cajun dishes from the Deep South
• **Ferryman's Tavern**: freshly brewed local beer and good pub food
• **Quaffers**: elegant wine bar, great oysters
• **Quay Four**: alfresco meals at the water's edge
• **Peers**: Sophisticated, sweeping views of harbour.

Left: *The Table Mountain cable car, with Lion's Head in the background; the mountain is a declared national monument.*

Above: *Elegant charm is the keynote of the Victoria and Alfred Waterfront; part of its attraction is that visitors can observe boats at work in the busy harbour.* **Opposite:** *The Victoria Wharf warehouse shelters a myriad speciality shops.*

The Waterfront ★★★

City and harbour, after a long separation, are being happily reunited by the ambitious **Victoria and Alfred Waterfront** redevelopment scheme, a multibillion-dollar private venture that has borrowed ideas from San Francisco's harbour project, Boston's Quincy Market and others, but retains a lively character of its own. Among its various attractions are restaurants, bistros and bars, speciality shops, craft, fish and produce markets, cinemas and entertainment centres, hotels and museums (including a maritime expo). Under construction, or planned, are a yacht basin and marina, a world-class oceanarium – a great white shark will be one of the attractions – and waterways (a canal will lead into the city). For all that, though, it's a lived-in, workaday area as well as a fun place: fishing boats still use it (some now do duty as tourist craft); office and residential complexes are going up. It's highly recommended to visitors, though it gets rather crowded (and the service rushed) over weekends and public holidays.

Bo-Kaap ★

This inner suburb, on the lower slopes of **Signal Hill** west of the central area, is a colourful splash of exotic culture in an otherwise standard city setting: a picturesque place of mosques and quaint flat-roofed little 18th-century houses, and home to part of Cape Town's **Islamic** community, many of whom are descended from Indonesian slaves and political exiles brought in by the early Dutch colonists. The name in translation means 'above Cape', though it is also known as the **Malay Quarter**. There's a small museum – a period house – *in situ* at 71 Wale Street. We suggest you don't wander around on your own, but rather take in the Bo-Kaap as part of an organized tour (contact Tasneem Kalam, tel: (021) 408-7231 or 26-1977).

Please note: there's a lot of poverty and unemployment in the city and surrounds, and muggings are a risk. Take the basic precautions. Strolling along well-used roads is safe enough in daylight hours, safer in company.

> **RHODES MEMORIAL**
>
> This tribute to 19th-century financier and visionary **Cecil Rhodes**, situated on the eastern slopes of Devil's Peak, was designed in grandly classical style as a 'temple' by the celebrated architect **Herbert Baker**. Kipling's farewell words to the 'immense and brooding spirit' are inscribed on a bust of Rhodes; G. F. Watts' splendid statue of **'Physical Energy'** is also part of the complex, which has a pleasant tearoom attached.

Shopping

Cape Town is the place to shop for contemporary African art and artefacts, curios, gold and diamond jewellery (which is tax free), ethnic jewellery, leatherware and clothing (South Africa has a sophisticated clothing industry and boasts some top designers).

There are also plenty of antiques on offer but beware of tourist traps; try **Long Street** and the **Church Street** open-air antique fair (open on Fridays). For Africana you can't go wrong at **Clarke's Bookshop** in Long Street.

Permanent open-air markets in the city at **Greenmarket Square**, **St George's Mall**, the **Grand Parade** and the railway station offer fun shopping. You are likely to find a lot of junk, some good buys and, occasionally, a real bargain.

Sophisticated shoppers should visit the **Golden Acre** in Adderley Street, **St George's Mall**, **Stuttaford's Town Centre**, the **V&A Waterfront**, and, in Claremont, stylish **Cavendish Square** and the adjacent **Link** complex.

SUNSET CRUISES

- **Alabama 2000**: daily harbour cruise with dinner, dancing and cabaret show; tel: (021) 419-3122.
- **Circe Launch**: sunset trip from Hout Bay to Cape Town harbour; sparkling wine and snacks; runs Oct to Apr; return bus trip available; tel: (021) 790-1040.
- **Sealink Tours**: cruise from Waterfront to Clifton; sparkling wine and souvenir champagne glass; runs Dec to Mar; tel: (021) 25-4480.

BEST BEACHES

Much of the coastline is ideal for bathing, boating, surfing, sailing, fishing – and sun worshipping. The western waters (**Camps Bay**, glamorous **Clifton**, pretty **Llandudno**, and **Sandy Bay** for nudists) are exceedingly chilly but the beaches are generally sheltered from the prevailing summer southeaster and are much favoured by sun lovers. **Hout Bay** and **Noordhoek** are both lovely. On the eastern side it tends to be windy but the sea is warmer (**Muizenberg**, **Froggy Pond**, **Fish Hoek**). **Boulders** (don't miss its jackass penguins!) and **St James** tend to be protected from the wind. These beaches are crowded during holiday season so you would be wise to make an early start. Up the west coast is **Bloubergstrand**, popular for surfing and boardsailing competitions.

Cape Peninsula

Highlights of what the Cape Peninsula has to offer are a leisurely drive around the Peninsula's coastline (for which you should set aside a day), the botanical gardens at Kirstenbosch, and Constantia's wine estates. A visit to the last two can either become part of your day tour, or be undertaken as separate excursions.

Drive southwards along the coastal road from Sea Point to picturesque Llandudno, passing Bantry Bay, Clifton and Camps Bay (the imposing **Twelve Apostles**, an extension of the Table Mountain range, line the route on your left), and then on to the fishing harbour of Hout Bay. Continue over the spectacular **Chapman's Peak Drive** to Noordhoek and Kommetjie, where you bear right for the **Cape of Good Hope Nature Reserve** and **Cape Point**. Then travel back along the east coast, past Boulders and Seaforth, through Simon's Town (steeped in naval history) and, finally, Muizenberg.

Cape Point ★★★

Cape Point, at the tip of the Peninsula, is known as the meeting place of two oceans and Africa's second most southerly extremity after **Cape Agulhas**. For breathtaking views from its high promontory, you can walk up the steep roadway or take the shuttle bus.

It is off Cape Point that sightings of *The Flying Dutchman*, a legendary phantom ship, have been reported. The legend originated in the 17th century with the foundering of Dutch captain Hendrick van der Decken's ship in stormy seas. Vowing that he would round the **Cape of Good Hope** if it took him till Doomsday, fate pinned him to his promise.

The headland is part of the extensive Cape of Good Hope Nature Reserve, a place of marvellous floral diversity (seen at its best in the spring months) and a sanctuary for various antelope. The local baboons tend to be overfriendly (don't feed or tease them). Facilities in the reserve include swimming, fishing and barbecue spots, and a restaurant and gift shop. There is also a selection of hiking paths (maps are supplied at the entrance gate); of note is a short trail from Olifantsbos, skirting rock pools and leading to the wreck of the *Thomas T. Tucker*.

HOUT BAY

This charming residential and fishing centre on the Peninsula's west coast lies in a lovely valley bounded by wooded mountain slopes. Besides its beach, attractions include the picturesque harbour and its **Mariner's Wharf** (with a fresh fish market and restaurants) and the **World of Birds,** southern Africa's largest bird park (with landscaped walk-through aviaries). The small **Hout Bay Museum** often organizes interesting walks.

Opposite: *Llandudno Beach fringes the most charming of the Peninsula's seaside villages.* **Below:** *Cape Point rises majestically above the southern ocean.*

Kirstenbosch National Botanical Gardens ★★★

On the hillside below the Table Mountain range, above the fashionable suburb of **Newlands**, Kirstenbosch ranks among the world's most celebrated botanic gardens. An astonishing array of flowering plants (around one quarter of the country's 24,000 species) are cultivated here: proteas, pelargoniums, ericas, mesembryanthemums, ferns, cycads of ancient origin and much else. The herbarium houses over 300,000 specimens; there are delightful walks along the many pathways; the birdlife is enchanting, and the restaurant serves unpretentious but sustaining food. On summer weekends, champagne breakfasts are popular (bring your own bubbly), as are the Sunday-evening concerts; pack a picnic. Check the newspapers for concert details.

Constantia Wine Estates ★★★

There are three of these in the exquisite valley that cuts through the central Peninsula and together they form the local 'wine route'. **Groot Constantia**, the oldest and stateliest of the homesteads, dates from the late 17th century and is notable for its architecture, period furniture, two-storeyed wine cellar, museum and lovely grounds (the oak-lined avenue leads to an ornamental pool). For visitors there are daily wine sales, with some superlative vintages on offer, cellar tours, a horse and carriage for hire, picnic lunches on the pretty, shaded lawns and three restaurants.

 Klein Constantia is smaller, rather more private, and **Buitenverwachting** has a restaurant that's regularly voted one of the country's best. Not to be missed are the summer concerts (jazz and classical music) on Buitenverwachting's great lawn girded by giant oaks and vineyards. Ticket prices include a bottle of the estate's excellent wine, but bring your own picnic; watch the newspaper for details.

 Make sure you visit the nearby **Old Cape Farm Stall** for high-quality South African fruits, preserves and a tantalizing range of gourmet delicacies. The atmospheric, reed-ceilinged **Coffee Shop** next door is highly fashionable for late weekend breakfasts (booking is essential) and light, country-style lunches.

THE WINELANDS

The winelands of the Cape comprise a region of grand mountain ranges, fertile valleys, vineyards and orchards heavy with fruit, and of homesteads built in the distinctive and gracious style known as **Cape Dutch**. These were the first rural areas to be taken over by the early white colonists: they began infiltrating the traditional Khoisan lands of the interior in the 1660s, turning the countryside over to pasture, the growing of wheat and, increasingly, the cultivation of wine grapes. The farms prospered, the colony expanded, and towns were founded: **Stellenbosch** in 1679, **Franschhoek** (French glen, named in honour of its Huguenot origins) 10 years later, to be followed by **Paarl, Wellington, Tulbagh, Worcester, Robertson** and others, all of them worth visiting for their history and the beauty of their surrounds.

For visitors to this lovely region of many moods and faces, each season has its enchantment. In high summer the orchards and vineyards are laden with fruit, the air hot and heavy with the scents of the harvest; in autumn the colours change to create a symphony of russets and golds, and farm trucks bear great loads of sweet-smelling grapes to the pressing rooms. Snow covers the high mountain peaks in winter; spring carpets the valleys and slopes with a profusion of wild flowers.

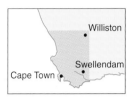

Opposite: *Along one stretch the main coastal road running south from Cape Town to Cape Point cuts through Chapman's Peak, from which there are breathtaking views of the sea 600 m (2,000 ft) below and, in the distance, the picturesque fishing harbour of Hout Bay and its backing mountains.* **Below:** *An enchanting corner of Stellenbosch, historic 'capital' of the Cape Winelands.*

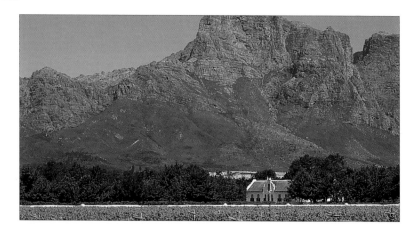

Above: *Boschendal, one of the winelands' beautiful and historic estates, embodies the Cape Flemish style and dates from 1812.*

POINTS OF INTEREST IN AND AROUND STELLENBOSCH

** **Oude Libertas Centre**: stunning setting for open-air music, opera and drama (picnicking permitted on shaded lawns). Check newspaper for details.
* **Oude Meester Brandy Museum**: fascinating insights into past and present.
* **Bergkelder**: the cellars have been carved out of the hillside.
* **Van Ryn Brandy Cellar**, near Vlottenberg (closed weekends): entices visitors with musical events and a fun train trip offering brandy cocktails and brunch.

Stellenbosch ★★★

Most historic of the wineland towns, Stellenbosch is less than an hour's drive from Cape Town; it lies in the Eerste River valley beneath the Papegaaiberg. Founded in the late 17th century, the place grew graciously to maturity, its dappled oak-lined streets fringed by some lovely old buildings, the best of which can be seen the length of **Dorp Street**, around **Die Braak** (the village green) and in the **Village Museum** collection. The latter is a cluster of beautifully restored historic houses from different eras, furnished in period style and embraced by a re-creation of the graceful gardens that must have existed in earlier times. Among them are **Schreuder House** (1709), believed to be South Africa's oldest surviving town house; the gabled **Blettermanhuis** (1760-90); **Grosvenor House** (1800-30) and the **House of O.M. Bergh** (1840-70).

Stellenbosch is a leading centre of learning; university and town are harmoniously integrated. It is also the starting point of a major wine route: 20 estates and cellars are within a 12-kilometre (7 miles) radius.

Paarl ★

The biggest of the wineland towns, Paarl was founded in 1720 and named after the dome-shaped granite rock on the overlooking mountain (it reminded an early traveller of a giant pearl). The mountain and its surrounds are maintained as an attractive nature reserve; there's a circular route to the top; well worth a short digression is the **Mill Stream wildflower garden**.

Paarl's long main street is shaded by oaks and jacarandas; among features of interest in and around the area are the **KWV** complex – the world's largest wine cooperative – and its historic **Laborie** homestead; the **Wagonmakers museum**; the **Oude Pastorie**, an architectural gem which holds some fine old Cape furniture and silverware; and the **Taalmonument**, or Afrikaans Language Monument.

Not far out of Paarl is **Nederburg**, an elegant Cape Dutch homestead set in a wide sweep of countryside mantled by vines. The Nederburg wine auction, held around April each year, is a hugely social as well as an important business occasion.

Franschhoek ★★

This small centre, founded in 1688 on land granted to **Huguenot** refugees from a Europe plagued by religious strife, is set in an especially beautiful valley. Little remains of the original French culture except the names of the surrounding estates. The most notable features of

---

FRANSCHHOEK'S FORTÉ: FIRST-CLASS DINING

● **Le Quartier Français**, Huguenot Road: award-winner, exquisite French-influenced, Cape-style cuisine, tel: (02212) 2248.
● **La Petite Ferme**, Pass Road: sweeping views of the valley, great food, tel: (02212) 3016.
● **La Maison de Chamonix**, Uitkyk Road: voted among the country's top three popular restaurants, tel: (02212) 2393.
● **Chez Michel**, Huguenot Road: French bistro atmosphere, tel: (02212) 2671.
● **Polfyntjies**, fresh country cooking, tel: (02212) 3217.

Below: *The Huguenot Memorial honours the contribution made by the early French immigrants.*

SELECT WINE ESTATES

★★★ Boschendal: 17th-century Cape Flemish-style manor house; Capetonians flock here for lunch, a splendid buffet of traditional Cape fare. Picnic baskets provided in summer for those who like to eat under the pines in the grounds.

★★★ Fairview: makes variety of cheeses from estate's own goat's milk; gorgeous peacocks roam the gardens.

★★ Backsberg: tasting under the oaks in summer; self-guided cellar tours; small wine museum.

★★ Delheim: described as a 'tourist's jewel and photographer's paradise'.

★★ Blaauwklippen: charming, gabled house; museum; coach rides.

Above: *A vegetable and fruit stall near Robertson; the surrounding countryside boasts a dozen or so thoroughbred stud farms.*

Franschhoek are the first-class restaurants nestled in its vine-covered valley. The graceful **Huguenot Memorial** and its next-door museum complex stand at the end of the town's long main street.

The Wine Routes

The winelands are graced by some fine Cape Dutch country houses, products of a style that began to emerge in the early 1700s, drawing elements from both Holland and the Orient but evolving a distinctive character of its own. Most have a simple symmetry about them, many are gabled, a few are truly grand. They are also accessible to the tourist by way of the various wine routes in and around Stellenbosch, Franschhoek, Paarl, Worcester and

Robertson – a very pleasant way to spend one's day.

There are literally hundreds of wineries and estates, so visitors with limited time will be able to cover only a fraction of them. A visit to four or maybe five is the most you can expect to manage in a day's outing.

Most cellars offer tours (at set times) and tastings, and there's no limit to the number of wines you're allowed to try, though many of the places charge a small initial fee per glass. Some run excellent restaurants; at others there are farm stalls selling local specialities, gift shops, and sometimes galleries or museums.

DAY DRIVES FROM CAPE TOWN

Hermanus ★★★

From Cape Town, make your way through Somerset West along the main N2 highway which leads over the mountains, beyond which are the fruit orchards of Elgin and Grabouw, and on to the pretty cliffside town of Hermanus. Best known for its **southern right whales,** Hermanus has become quite a tourist attraction during the mid-winter months when these ponderous but oddly graceful mammals make their way into the bay to calve, their arrival heralded by the town's official **'whale crier'**. Excellent lunches are served by Hermanus's **Marine Hotel**, a place still run in the grand Victorian tradition. A more scenic drive, and only slightly longer, takes you along the coast from Gordon's Bay past Betty's Bay; the **Harold Porter Nature Reserve** here is worth a visit.

CAPE AGULHAS

Some 100 km (62 miles) to the east of Cape Town is Cape Agulhas, the southernmost point of the African continent. The name is derived from the Portuguese word for 'needles' (the early navigators found that their compasses here weren't affected by magnetic deviation). Completed in 1848, the **Cape Agulhas lighthouse** is the second oldest in South Africa, and has been declared a national monument. A lighthouse museum (the only one in the country) offers fascinating displays that trace lighthouse development from ancient times to the present.

Worth an hour of one's time is the **shipwreck museum** in nearby **Bredasdorp**.

Above: *Hiking in the scenically grand Hottentots-Holland mountains.*
Opposite, below: *The Old Harbour at Hermanus has been preserved as a museum, and as a tacit memorial to the hardy fishermen of yesteryear.*

Above: *Alfresco enjoyment at Melkbosskerm, one of the West Coast's marvellously informal outdoor seafood restaurants. The region is renowned for its crayfish.*
Opposite: *The springtime glory of Namaqualand.*

West Coast ★★

A pleasant excursion is that leading up the west coast to **Langebaan Lagoon**, one of the country's finest wetlands and a bird-watcher's paradise. Visit the **West Coast National Park** (headquarters at Langebaan Lodge), Langebaan village (boat trips, country club, Club Mykonos – a Greek-style entertainment and residential complex) and **Saldanha Bay** (seafood and boat trips).

Four Passes ★★

If you're in a motoring mood, the scenically splendid Four Passes drive leads you from Cape Town to Stellenbosch, and over the **Helshoogte Pass** which towers above the Drakenstein valley area. It then takes you past Boschendal Estate and Franschhoek (*see* p. 115), over the rugged **Franschhoek Pass** and through the apple orchards of Elgin and Grabouw, before bringing you home over the **Hottentots-Holland** range via **Sir Lowry's Pass** and through Somerset West.

If you feel inclined to taste a few wines, pay a visit to Anglo-American's new multimillion-rand wine cellar on the **Vergelegen Estate**. Designed by a Parisian architect, the winery is built into the hillside and offers a 360-degree view unequalled by any Cape wine farm. You can enjoy a light lunch or stay for tea; visits to the winery by appointment. Nature lovers shouldn't miss a visit to the nearby **Helderberg Nature Reserve**, which offers lovely scenery, as well as interesting flora and birdlife.

NAMAQUALAND – FLOWERING DESERT

At first sight the plains of Namaqualand, the arid western coastal strip that stretches up to the Orange River and Namibia in the north, seems too harsh and inhospitable to support any but the hardiest, least appealing kinds of life. Yet the region is unbelievably rich in succulents and flowering annuals. After the winter rains – between **late July** and **September** – the land is briefly and gloriously mantled by great carpets of wild flowers.

Namaqualand is home to about 4,000 different floral species, most of which belong to the daisy and mesembryanthemum (known locally as 'vygies') groups but there are also aloes and lilies, perennial herbs and a host of others. The small, low-growing plants are drought resistant, the seeds lying dormant during the long dry months. Then, after the winter rains but before the onset of the burning desert winds – when they sense the impending arrival of the pollinators – they burst into bright life, maturing in a matter of days to magically transform the countryside.

It's worth making the long journey to witness the spectacle. Organized tours are available; **Specialised Tours**, for instance, offer a day trip that embraces Langebaan Lagoon, Mamre and Darling; en route you're treated to a seafood lunch and, of course, to marvellous wildflower displays. For those who have the time, a longer three-day tour is recommended.

WHEN AND WHERE TO SEE FLOWERS

The best months are normally **Aug** to **Sep**, but as this varies from year to year, call Flowerline first, tel: (021) 418-3705 (or visit them at Captour).
• The most spectacular displays are normally in the **Postberg Nature Reserve**, around **Clanwilliam** and the **Biedouw Valley**, **Vanrhynsdorp**, **Nieuwoudtville**, **Kamieskroon** and **Springbok**.
• On sunny days flowers open between 10:00 and 16:30; on very overcast days they do not open at all.
• A flower tour can be accomplished in one day (for example, if you visit Postberg, near Langebaan), but allow two to three days for the major routes.
• If you set aside several days to view the flowers, choose private accommodation for a more personal touch, as the hotels are generally very average.
• Take warm clothing, as mornings and evenings can still be very chilly.

Cape Town and Surrounds at a Glance

Sep and **Oct** (spring): pleasant for the crisp air, spirit of reawakening and fynbos in flower; **Mar** and **Apr** (autumn) for balmy, still days that have lost their scorch.

Cape Town's **international airport** 22 km (14 miles) outside the city. Regular shuttle bus service links airport with Cape Town railway station (buses depart from main vehicle entrance, outside platform 24). To book contact Captour.

Entire length of eastern peninsula serviced by excellent **rail network**, linking southern suburbs to city. Timetables available from Captour. Waterfront linked to city centre by **shuttle bus**; leaves regularly from outside Information Bureau, Adderley St. Blue-and-yellow **Rikkis**, inexpensive roving cabs, also cater for small groups who like to devise their own fun tours, tel: (021) 23-4888. Most **car-hire** firms represented.

Cape Town
Mount Nelson, Gardens: one of the country's oldest and most elegant, tel: (021) 23-1000, fax: 24-7472.
Victoria & Alfred Waterfront Hotel, Pierhead: superb views of Table Bay, tel: (021) 419-6677, fax: 419-8955.

The Bay, Camps Bay seafront: pristinely modern, tel: (021) 438-4444, fax: 438-4455.
Cape Sun, central city, tel: (021) 23-8844, fax: 23-8875.
Cellars Country House, Constantia: originally an 18th-century wine cellar, tel: (021) 794-2137.
Vineyard Hotel, Newlands: historic hotel (1799), beautiful gardens, tel: (021) 64-2107, fax: 683-3365.

BUDGET ACCOMMODATION
Breakwater Lodge, Waterfront: good value, tel: (021) 406-1911, fax: 406-1070.
City Lodge (Mowbray and V&A Waterfront): tel: (021) 419-9450, fax: 419-0460.
Holiday Inn Garden Courts: De Waal, Greenmarket Square, St George's Mall, Newlands, call toll free 0800-117711.

Stellenbosch
D'Ouwe Werf, 30 Church St: small, historic and charming, tel: (021) 887-4608, fax: 887-4626.
The **Lanzerac**, Lanzerac Rd: gracious historic estate, tel: (021) 887-1132, fax: 887-2310.
L'Auberge Rozendal, Omega Rd, Jonkershoek: on working wine farm, tel: (021) 883-8737,

Paarl
Grande Roche, Plantasie St: luxury hotel set amongst terraced vineyards; plush, offers

international standards, tel: (02211) 63-2727, fax: 63-2220.
Mountain Shadows, off Klein Drakenstein Road: inviting country house, tel: (02211) 62-3192, fax: 62-6796.
Roggeland country house, Noorder-Paarl: charming, superb cuisine, tel: (02211) 68-2501, fax: 68-2113.

Franschhoek
L'Auberge du Quartier Français, cnr Berg and Wilhelmina sts: delightful setting, maintains superb international quality, tel: (02212) 2151, fax: 3105.
Le Ballon Rouge, Reservoir St East: restored Victorian guest house, seven rooms each named after red grape cultivar, tel: (02212) 2651.

Somerset West
Lord Charles Hotel, cnr Stellenbosch and Faure rds: luxurious, tel: (024) 51-2970, fax: 55-1107

Cape Town
Blues, Camps Bay: California-style, overlooks palm-fringed shore, tel: (021) 438-2040.
Buitenverwachting, Constantia: one of the very best; chic, innovative cuisine, tel: (021) 794-3522.
Champers, Deer Park Drive, city: Swiss influence, artistic detail, tel: (021) 45-4335.
Constantia Uitsig, Uitsig Farm: set among wine estates, tel: (021) 794-6500.

Cape Town and Surrounds at a Glance

Fisherman's Cottage, Plumstead: charming cottage, cuisine using freshest ingredients, tel: (021) 797-6341.
Floris Smit Huijs, city centre: stylish, very fine food, tel: (021) 23-3414.
Jacksons, Peninsula hotel: imaginative dishes from around the world, tel: (021) 439-888.
Leinster Hall, Gardens: stately house, classic French cuisine, tel: (021) 24-1836.

Ethnic restaurants
Africa Café, Observatory: dishes from Cameroon, Kenya, Zambia and Mozambique, tel: (021) 47-9553.
Biesmiellah, Bo-Kaap: traditional Cape Malay food, no alcohol permitted, tel: (021) 23-0850.
Kaapse Tafel, Gardens: reliably good, traditional Cape cuisine, tel: (021) 23-1651.

Stellenbosch
De Kelder: built in 1790, traditional Cape dishes, tel: (021) 88-3797.
De Volkskombuis: delectable traditional cuisine, tel: (021) 887-2121.
Doornbosch: revamped, specializes in superb Italian fare; tel: (021) 887-5079.
Lord Neethling: historical monument, Oriental dishes, tel: (021) 883-8966.

Paarl
Bosman's, Grande Roche Hotel: best in the country, tel: (02211) 63-2727.

Rhebokskloof: wine estate with three restaurants, small lake featuring black swans, tel: (02211) 63-8606.
Troubadour: Swiss cuisine, Victorian house, tel: (02211) 63-3556.

Franschhoek
See p. 115.

Somerset West
Garden Terrace, Lord Charles Hotel: superb Cape Malay dishes, tel: (024) 55-1040.
L'Auberge du Paysan: top award-winner for French cuisine, tel: (024) 42-2008.

Tours and Excursions

Balloon tours over winelands (plus champagne): Wineland Ballooning, tel: (02211) 4-138.
Canoeing in the winelands: Felix Unite River Adventures, tel: (021) 762-6935; River Rafters, tel: (021) 72-5094.
Coach tours around Peninsula, Winelands and up West Coast: Hylton Ross, Mother City Tours, Windward Tours, Tailormade Tours, Specialised Tours; call Captour.
Off-the-beaten-track tours: Eco Explorers, tel: (021)

92-9361, Which Way Adventures, tel: (024) 2-2364.
Helicopter trips over Peninsula or Winelands: Civair, tel: (021) 948-8511, Court Helicopters, tel: (021) 25-2966.
Steam-train trips (Winelands and wildflower regions): contact Ian Gilmour, Cape Western Railway Preservation Trust, tel: (021) 64-2447.
Vineyard horse trails, Tailormade Tours, tel: (021) 64-4415.
Winelands (specialized tours): call Helen Frith of Vineyard Ventures, tel: (021) 419-1854; or Tailormade Tours, tel: (021) 64-4415.

Useful Contacts

Captour (car-hire and booking facilities, ecotourism, accommodation), railway station complex, off Adderley St, tel: (021) 418-5214.
Stellenbosch Tourist Information Bureau, tel: (02231) 83-3584.
Victoria & Alfred Waterfront Information Centre, tel: (021) 418-2369.
West Coast Tourism, Saldanha Bay: tel: (02281) 4-2088.

CAPE TOWN	J	F	M	A	M	J	J	A	S	O	N	D
AVERAGE TEMP. °F	70	70	69	63	58	55	54	55	57	61	64	68
AVERAGE TEMP. °C	21	21	20	17	15	13	12	13	14	16	18	20
Hours of Sun Daily	11	10	9	7	6	6	6	7	8	9	10	11
SEA TEMP. °F	59	57	55	55	54	54	54	55	55	57	57	67
SEA TEMP. °C	15	14	13	13	12	12	12	13	13	14	14	14
RAINFALL in	1	1	1	2	3	4	3	3	2	2	1	1
RAINFALL mm	14	17	19	39	74	92	70	75	39	37	15	17
Days of Rainfall	5	4	5	8	12	12	11	13	10	8	5	5

Travel tips

Tourist Information

Satour (the South African Tourism Board) maintains offices in, among other countries, the United Kingdom (London), the United States (New York and Los Angeles), France (Paris), Germany (Frankfurt), Israel (Tel Aviv), Italy (Milan), Japan (Tokyo), the Netherlands, Belgium and Scandinavia (principal office Amsterdam), Switzerland and Austria (principal office Zürich), Taiwan (Taipeh), and Zimbabwe (Harare).

Satour's headquarters are in the Menlyn Park office block, corner Atterbury Road and Menlyn Drive, Pretoria; Private Bag X164, Pretoria 0001; tel: (012) 47-1131 and (012) 348-9521. Regional offices are located in Bloemfontein, Cape Town, Durban, East London, George, Johannesburg (city and international airport), Kimberley, Nelspruit, Pietersburg and Port Elizabeth. Consult the local directories for addresses and telephone numbers.

Major centres and tourist areas have **publicity associations** which provide up-to-date information, free of charge, on everything from recreation to transport and accommodation. Contact addresses and numbers for many of these appear in the relevant chapters of this book. **Computicket**, which has branches countrywide, handles most concert, theatre and cinema bookings. For any information, call (021) 21-4715.

Entry Documents

All visitors need a valid passport for entry into South Africa. Most foreign nationals, however, are exempt from visa requirements, including citizens of the United States, Canada and the European Community, as well as the following countries: Australia, New Zealand, Japan, Namibia, Austria, Brazil, Chile, Botswana, Austria, Ireland, Singapore and Switzerland.

Health Requirements

Visitors from or passing through a yellow fever zone (most of tropical Africa and South America) must be able to produce a valid International Certificate of Vaccination. Air travellers who only pass through the airports of such a zone are exempt from the requirement. Note that cholera and smallpox certificates are no longer needed, and no Aids screening procedure is in force.

Air Travel

The country's major point of entry is Johannesburg's international airport, which also serves Pretoria. Durban and Cape Town airports have international status too. **Domestic services:** Among domestic centres served by South African Airways are Bloemfontein, Cape Town, Durban, East London, George, Johannesburg, Kimberley, Port Elizabeth, Pretoria and Upington. Comair and other small airlines serve the lesser towns and main tourist destinations.

Air charter services (including helicopter hire) are widely available.

Road Travel

South Africa has an extensive and well-signposted road network comprising some

200,000 kilometres (124,280 miles) of national and provincial highways. Surfaces are generally in very good condition, though the going can be a bit rugged in the remoter and hillier country areas.

Driver's licence: You must carry this with you at all times. Zimbabwe, Mozambique, Namibia, Botswana, Lesotho and Swaziland licences are valid in South Africa. So too are other foreign licences, provided they carry a photograph and are either printed in English or accompanied by an English-language certificate of authenticity.

Alternatively, obtain an International Driving Permit before your departure.

Road rules and signs: In South Africa, one drives on the left. The general speed limit on national highways, urban freeways and other major routes is 120 km/h (75 mph); that on secondary (rural) roads is 100 km/h (60 mph), and in built-up areas 60 km/h (35 mph) unless otherwise indicated.

Main roads are identified by colour and number rather than by name. Using a good map (one which incorporates the route marker system), the visitor should have little difficulty in finding his/her way around city and country.

Car hire: Avis, Imperial (incorporating Hertz), Budget and other, smaller, rental firms are well represented in the major centres. Airports and some of the bigger game parks (Kruger, Kalahari Gemsbok) have car-hire facilities.

ROAD SIGNS IN AFRIKAANS

Words to watch out for are:
Links (left)
Regs (right)
Stad (city)
Lughawe (airport)
Straat (street)
Weg (road)
Rylaan (avenue)
Hou (keep)
Slegs (only)
Oop (open)
Gesluit (closed)
Gevaar (beware hazard)
Verbode (forbidden)
Ompad (detour)
Tuin ('garden' but often used in conjunction with 'wild' – e.g. **wildtuin** – to denote a park or reserve)
Strand (beach)
Hawe (harbour).
Note that in South Africa a 'robot' is a set of traffic lights.

Insurance: Your motor vehicle must be covered by a Third Party Insurance policy; if you're hiring a car, the rental firm will make the appropriate arrangements; for overland visitors, insurance tokens are available at Beitbridge and other major border control posts.

Maps: Excellent regional and city maps are available from Satour, the Automobile Association, from major book stores and airport kiosks. Recommended are those in the Map Studio series.

Petrol: Cities, towns and main routes are very well served by filling stations. Many of these stay open 24 hours a day, others from 06:00 to 18:00. Petrol, either Super or Premium, is sold in litres. Note that on the Highveld, because of its altitude, the petrol has a lower octane rating (Super is 93, Premium 87; while on the coast, Super is 97 and Premium 93). Make sure you stick with Super or Premium rather than octane rating. Pump attendants see to your fuel and other needs.

Automobile Association: The AA is the country's biggest motoring club, and provides a wide range of services, including assistance with breakdowns and other emergencies, accommodation reservations and advice on touring, caravanning, camping, places of interest, insurance and car hire. Maps and brochures are available. These services are offered to visitors who belong to the AA or any affiliated motoring organization. The AA's headquarters are in AA House, 66 Korte Street, Braamfontein (Johannesburg) 2001; tel: (011) 407-1000. For AA offices in other centres, consult the relevant telephone directory.

Coach travel: Luxury coach services link the major centres (Greyhound, Intercape Ferreira, Translux, Trancity); tour operators spread the network wider, taking in game parks, scenic attractions and other tourist venues. For details, consult your travel agent or the local publicity association.

Clothes: What to Pack

South Africa enjoys long hot summers and generally mild winters; people dress informally, though 'smart casual' wear is often required after dark at theatres and other art/entertainment venues, and by the more sophisticated hotels and restaurants. Beach wear is acceptable only on the beach; casual clothing is customary at holiday resorts and in the game areas.

For the summer months (October to April), pack lightweight garments and a hat but include a jacket or jersey for the cooler, and occasionally chilly, nights. Most of the country is in the summer-rainfall zone, so bring an umbrella or raincoat. For the winter months, pack warm clothing.

Money Matters

The South African currency unit is the Rand, divided into 100 cents. Coins are issued in denominations of 1c, 2c, 5c, 10c, 20c, 50c, R1 and R2; notes in denominations of R5, R10, R20, R50, and recently, R100. Coinage designs were also recently changed, and some denominations circulate in two forms; beware the superficial similarity between the old 20c and the new R2 coin.

Currency exchange: Foreign currency can be converted into rands at banks, bureaux de change and through such authorized dealers as Thomas Cook and American Express.
Banks: Normal banking hours in major centres are 09:00 to 15:30 on weekdays and 08:30 or 09:00 to 11:00 on Saturdays. There are currency exchange and banking facili-

ties at the three international airports. Traveller's cheques may be cashed at any bank and at many hotels and shops.
Credit cards: Most hotels, restaurants, shops, car-hire companies and tour operators accept international credit cards (American Express, Bank of America, Visa, Diners Club, MasterCharge). Note that you cannot buy petrol with a credit card; some banks, however, issue a special 'Petrocard'.
Value Added Tax: VAT, currently at 14 per cent, is levied on most goods (basic foodstuffs are exempt); foreign visitors can claim back the tax paid on goods to be taken out of the country and whose total value exceeds R250. For this you'll need to present (at the point of exit) your passport, the goods themselves and the relevant invoices.
Tipping: Provided the service is satisfactory, it's usual to tip porters, waiters/waitresses, taxi drivers, room attendants and golf caddies. Tipping petrol attendants is optional, though a window-wash and a cheerful smile merit recognition. Gratuities for quantifiable services (waiters, taxi drivers) should amount to at least 10 per cent of the cost of the service; for nonquantifiable services of a minor nature (porterage, for example) it's customary to offer a tip of around R2.
Service charges: Hotels may not by law levy a charge for general services (though there's often a telephone ser-

vice loading, sometimes a hefty one). Restaurants may levy such a charge; few do so.

Accommodation

A voluntary grading system, covering all types of accommodation, was recently introduced; ratings range from one to five stars.

The best South African hotels are of international standard but, generally speaking, local hoteliers still have a lot to learn from their counterparts in Europe, North America and the Pacific Rim. Major groups are **Sun International** (casino hotels), **Southern Sun/Holiday Inns**, **Karos** and **Protea**. Most of them fall into the middle price range, but Protea establishments tend to retain a more individual character, and offer quality and good value.

Rather than visitors restricting their options to the major hotel chains, it is recommended that they choose some of the country getaways and guest farms (which we have tended to highlight throughout this book). There is a great variety of secluded, restful guest houses often close to the major tourist areas (Eastern Transvaal, Northern Natal, the Garden Route, the Cape Peninsula, Winelands and West Coast). You're assured of good food and personal service.

The larger South African game parks and reserves (run by the **National Parks Board**, tel: (012) 343-1991, and those in Natal by the **Natal Parks Board**, tel:

(0331) 47-1961), offer comfortable, mainly self-catering accommodation in fully equipped chalets, bungalows, cottages and less sophisticated huts, though many rest camps also boast an à la carte restaurant.

It is worth noting that these two controlling bodies play a very important role in the conservation of the country's national parks, while aiming for a sensitive balance between ecology and material benefit to neighbouring impoverished communities.

Game lodges are an increasingly prominent feature in the South African hospitality business. Usually located in private game reserves and on game farms, these cater largely for fairly affluent people who like to live well while they explore the ways of the wild; most lodges pride themselves on the degree of personal attention lavished on each guest, and on the skill of their rangers and trackers.

Self-catering options are varied and numerous, ranging from the rudimentary hiking hut through holiday apartments and cottages to the well-appointed, even luxurious, resort chalet.

Bed-and-breakfast accommodation is becoming increasingly popular, and many residents in the major tourist areas are making their homes available to visitors; for those who enjoy a warmer and more personal touch, this type of accommodation is ideal.

For detailed information, consult a travel agent, Satour or the relevant regional publicity association.

Trading Hours

At the time of writing these were subject to review and change; Sunday trading hours, in particular, are likely to become a lot less restrictive. Normal shopping and business hours are 08:30 to 17:00 Mondays to Fridays and 08:30 to 13:00 on Saturdays. However, many of the larger supermarkets and the more enterprising shopping complexes close later on weekdays and stay open on Saturday afternoons, Sunday mornings and over public holidays.

Bars usually open at 10:00 and close at 23:00 on weekdays and Saturdays; nightclubs and some city bars remain open until 02:00 or later on weekdays.

Public Holidays

At the time of writing, these were under review; in 1993 there were 11 public holidays: New Year's Day (1 January), Good Friday, Family Day (Easter Monday), Founders' Day (6 April), Workers' Day (1 May), Ascension Day (9 May), Republic Day (31 May), Kruger Day (10 October), Day of the Vow (16 December), Christmas Day (25 December) and the Day of Goodwill (26 December).

Soweto Day (16 June) is regarded as a commemorative day by large numbers of South Africans.

The Jewish, Hindu and Islamic communities observe their traditional holy days.

Measurements

South Africa uses the metric system.

Telephones

The telecommunications system is almost fully automatic; one can dial direct to most centres in South (and southern) Africa and to most parts of the world. Telephone directories list the dialling codes; facsimile transmission (fax) facilities are widely available. **Enquiries:** Should you find that a number you need is not listed in the telephone directory, or the number has changed, dial 1023.

CONVERSION CHART		
FROM	TO	MULTIPLY BY
Millimetres	inches	0·0394
Metres	yards	1·0936
Metres	feet	3·281
Kilometres	miles	0·6214
Hectares	acres	2·471
Litres	pints	1·760
Kilograms	pounds	2·205
Tonnes	tons	0·984
To convert Celsius to Fahrenheit: $\times 9 \div 5 + 32$		

Time

Throughout the year, South African Standard Time is two hours ahead of Greenwich Mean (or Universal Standard) Time, one hour ahead of Central European Winter Time, and seven hours ahead of the USA's Eastern Standard Winter Time.

Electricity

Generally, urban power systems are 220/230 volts AC at 50 cycles a second; Pretoria's system generates 250 volts; Port Elizabeth's 220/250 volts. Plugs are 5-amp 2-pin or 15-amp 3-pin (round pins). Not all electric shavers will fit hotel and game-park plug points; visitors should seek advice about adaptors from a local electrical supplier.

Water

South Africa is one of the few countries in the world where the tap water is extremely palatable and perfectly safe to drink.

Medical Services

Visitors are responsible for their own medical arrangements, and are urged to take out medical insurance before departure. Private doctors are listed in the telephone directory under **'Medical Practitioners'**. Hospital admissions are usually arranged through a private practitioner, but in an emergency a visitor may telephone or go directly to the casualty department of a General Hospital or, in the smaller centres, to any public medical facility. Hospitals are listed under 'H' in the telephone directory.

Health Hazards

Malaria: The disease is largely but not completely under control in South Africa; still-risky regions are the Northern and Eastern Transvaal, Northern Natal and Zululand. If you're planning to visit one of these areas, embark on a course of anti-malaria tablets before starting out. Tablets are available without prescription from local pharmacies. Note that some strains of this disease are becoming immune to chloroquine (the most common anti-malarial drug) so rather use a substitute prophylactic.

Bilharzia: Also known as schistosomiasis, this debilitating waterborne disease is caused by a parasitical worm common in the lower-lying northern and eastern regions. Be circumspect about swimming in rivers and dams unless the assurances are clear that they are bilharzia free.

Aids: Although the incidence of full-blown Aids in South Africa remained low during the early 1990s, the disease is likely to reach critical proportions. The risk of contracting Aids, however, is no greater here than in any other country, provided that the standard and well-publicized precautions are taken.

Creepy crawlies: South Africa has its fair share of snakes, spiders, scorpions and sundry stinging insects, but surprisingly few travellers, even those on safari, suffer serious attack or even discomfort. However, those holidaying in the bush, or on walking trails, should obviously be more wary, and follow the advice of their ranger or group leader. For protection against ticks (the small red, hard-backed one can transmit tick-bite fever), wear long pants on walks through long grass; apply insect repellant to bare legs and arms.

Emergencies

The national number for an ambulance is 10-177; for the police flying squad, 10-111. The national all-purpose emergency number, 107 (equivalent of the USA's 911), should only be used if the caller believes life, limb or property is threatened.

Among personal crisis help services are **Lifeline** and **Alcoholics Anonymous**; both are listed in the telephone directory.

Security

The transition to a fully democratic order in South Africa has in many ways proved traumatic; there is a great deal of poverty around, and the crime rate in some areas is high. Take the same precautions as you would, say, in central New York; don't walk alone at night in either city or suburb; avoid deserted and poorer areas, unless you're with a conducted group; don't carry large sums of cash around with you; don't leave valuables in your room (use the hotel's safety deposit box).

INDEX